THE 24 x 7 MARRIAGE

Vijay Nagaswami is a psychiatrist who has worked closely on relationships and with couples from all parts of the country for 25 years. He is a writer, columnist and author of two books, this being his third. He lives and works in Chennai. He can be contacted at vnagaswami@gmail.com

THE 24 x 7 MARRIAGE

Smart Strategies for Good Beginnings

VIJAY NAGASWAMI

westland

westland ltd

Venkat Towers, 165, P.H. Road, Maduravoyal, Chennai 600 095
No. 38/10 (New No.5), Raghava Nagar, New Timber Yard Layout, Bangalore 560 026
Survey No. A - 9, II Floor, Moula Ali Industrial Area, Moula Ali, Hyderabad 500 040
23/181, Anand Nagar, Nehru Road, Santacruz East, Mumbai 400 055
47, Brij Mohan Road, Daryaganj, New Delhi 110 002

First published by westland ltd, 2008

12 11 10 9 8 7 5

ISBN: 978-81-89975-79-1

Typeset in High Tower Text by SÜRYA, New Delhi
Printed at Sri Krishna Printers, Noida.

For,
Bobby and Nat, who were
and
Ruth and Keshava, who are

Contents

Acknowledgements

I guess only a writer can understand the sense of relief experienced when a book is finally done. Accompanying this is a sense of general well-being and a feeling of gratitude to pretty much the whole world, for facilitating the process of writing it. There are many people I would like to thank for this book, but owing to constraints of space, I am compelled to confine myself to expressing my most sincere thanks to the shortlist:

The innumerable couples who did and continue to do me the signal honour of sharing so completely and trustingly their life stories with me. I have learned much from them and their dignity.

The readers of my columns and books, who are willing to pay hard-earned money to either read what I have to say or give away my books as wedding gifts, because they believe in them.

Nilanjana Roy of Westland Ltd., who charmed me into writing this book, even when it was less than a germ of an idea, never losing her good cheer as I missed deadline after deadline, and Gautam Padmanabhan, CEO of Westland Ltd., whose quiet but reassuring presence does much more for an author than he knows.

Prita Maitra, my editor, who, aside from being terrific at what she does, is an unqualified joy to work with and a wonderfully supportive human being.

Sushila Ravindranath, my erstwhile editor at the *New Indian Express*, Chennai, who gave me the space and warm encouragement to share my thoughts, and Aditya Sinha, Editor-in-Chief, *New Indian Express*, Chennai, for granting me permission to reproduce some of what has appeared in my column, in modified form, in different places in the book.

And Usha, for not merely staying married to me for over 20 years, but also being my marital arts learning companion, the first reader of everything I've ever written (including this), my nurturer and the custodian of my mental health.

1.

In Search of the
Happy Marriage

Now that you have tied the knot—or decided that you are ready to tie the knot—you are gently floating along in the belief that your life has entered a new and wondrous state that you are determined to enjoy and get the most out of. People you know who are already married will tell you to enjoy it for as long as it lasts, and those around you who are single, will envy you this 'period' of magic.

Let me tell you that whatever joy and enchantment you experience in the early days of marriage need not disappear as your marriage progresses, even though people around you imply that it will. The magic of togetherness that you feel today will be replaced by an enduring feeling of connectedness over the years to come, if you configure your marriage well. What I am trying to say is that marriage can be a charmed institution, if we pay some attention to laying its foundations. It won't get built by itself; we need to build it. However, building our marriage need not be such a tiresome or burdensome thing to do, if we get our basics right. If we approach our marriage consciously and tweak things around a bit, we can get much more out of it than our parents or friends did.

For almost three decades, a question that I have been frequently asked is, '*Is there such a thing as a happy marriage?*' Initially, this question used to sadden me, for I believed it to be an indicator that most people were not really happy with their marital lives. However, after working closely with a wide cross-section of couples, whether married, living together or just dating, I came to realise that it merely represented the consternation and, sometimes, frustration, experienced by two people who had either made, or were in the process of making, a commitment to spending the rest of their lives together. The fact that they were struggling to find the right answers told me they were still looking for them, and this relieved me no end, since I am a firm believer that marriage is better designed to enhance the quality of life than detract from it. However, that people are floundering in their pursuit of that holy grail of marriage—bliss—is a hard fact of modern life and something that needs to be addressed in order that the country's Family Courts are not any more burdened than they currently are.

One undeniable fact of modern life is that couples do not seem to be trying hard enough to keep their marriages going. Tolerance is unfortunately not a virtue in contemporary marriages. This does not mean that couples do not try to get their marriage up and running. They do, of course, but they tend to give up too easily. One of the principal reasons why more marriages are not lasting the distance today is that the institution of marriage is changing and we are refusing to either recognise or accept this. Young people today are being pushed to performing marital roles that their lifestyles, environmental conditioning and thought processes do not equip them to understand, leave alone accept. The roles that their parents played— even if not with aplomb, at least with resigned conviction—are no longer feasible in the modern marriage. The more we deny this reality, the longer will the problem continue to bedevil us. What is urgently needed is for people engaging in married life to understand what they need to do to get the best out of it. Put differently, they need to understand that, just as in corporate life smart work yields better results than hard work, so too is the case in married life.

I have also noticed that the last couple of years have seen the emergence of a new type of service-provider: the 'marriage educator' or the 'marriage coach'. Whether or not this kind of service helps is too early to tell, but the fact that it exists at all is an indicator of how actively couples are seeking solutions. So, if anybody tries to tell you that marriage is no longer a relevant institution, don't give credence to it. Just look at any matrimonial website or classified advertisements in the matrimonial sections of newspapers and you will be reassured that large numbers of divorced people of both genders are seeking remarriage. Even if their first marriage has failed, they want to get married again. In other words, *the institution of marriage is not the problem, we are.* And if we are to get the best out of the institution, we need to look inside ourselves for the answers. Needless to add, this is easier said than done. Often, when we look hard into our own minds for these answers, we realise that even more questions present themselves. This happens largely because we lack a map to give us at least a couple of starting coordinates with which to begin our search.

It is to provide a few coordinates that I chose to write this book. While nobody should actually attempt to write a 'primer' or a 'manual' for marriage, since there are far too many variations in individual marriages, one can at least attempt to set out a few principles that may actually help us get things right. A rough road map, as it were. And hopefully, when a couple starting off on married life reads this, they will be able to find it easier to steer their marriage in the direction they are comfortable with rather than in the direction they are being exhorted to by forces around them. I would expect that this book would be more suitable for couples in the early years of their marriage, preferably during the first year, for this is when the foundations of marriage are usually laid.

That apart, what the reader may expect to get out of this book is a different way to look at marriage and how this understanding can help both partners format their relationship in a manner that works well for them. Also, the reader may be able to identify with some, if not all, of the stories that represent the experiences of newly married couples from different parts of the country. Needless to say, the stories are all fictionalised composites. By this I mean there's usually some basis to the experience narrated, but the identities of the people have been protected by fictionalising the events described. Also, I might add, I use the term *marriage* to refer to any committed relationship between two people—usually a man and a woman (the dynamics in gay and lesbian relationships are a bit different and are worthy of being described more specifically elsewhere)—whether or not the couple has gone through a legally or religiously binding ritual. In fact, many of the issues described might well apply to couples who are still dating.

However, I need to tell you that if you're looking for a well-developed algorithm for marriage, you will not find it in this book. I do not intend for the book to provide off-the-shelf, ready-to-implement solutions guaranteed to fix all your marital problems. In fact, no book, however well written, can do this. I would imagine that the way to get the best out of a book such as this is to read it a chapter at a time, introspect a bit, see whether and how the insights you obtain relate to your own situation, have a discussion with your partner, and then decide whether or not both of you would like to change your thinking and behaviour on the subject covered by the chapter. And in the process you are very likely to discover that yours, too, can be what most contemporary young Indians aspire to—a smart marriage.

2

The Smart Marriage

Arundhati, a 28-year-old copywriter in a small ad agency, was conflicted. On the one hand, she was keen to settle down and start a family, something she had always dreamed of. She also knew whom she wanted to do this with. Her childhood sweetheart, Raj, had recently come back into her life and they had, after a few dates, both realised that they still felt good about each other. Marriage was a natural extension of their feelings and they had discussed it several times, always with great enthusiasm. All the women in her social environment were married and seemed to be quite happy in their marriages from whatever she could see. Her conflict came about after she attended a talk by a prominent women's rights activist, whom she admired greatly. The lady had warned all those listening to her that marriage was not a state that one entered lightly into. She had highlighted some of the terrible things that could and had happened to people who were married. That she herself was happily married, she attributed to a lot of effort by both her husband and herself. 'If you do get married,' she exhorted her audience, 'be prepared to work hard on your marriage'.

Naturally, this spooked Arundhati and possibly many other young women in the audience, but, in truth, until about a decade-and-a-half ago, I thought along pretty much the same lines as the lady activist. But with increasing personal experience I have come to realise that hard work doesn't necessarily get one very far. Actually, the thought of hard work on one's marriage can be a little off-putting, particularly when one hopes for spontaneity, fun and happiness, when one gets married. In my experience, I have found that the term 'hard work' means different things to different people. In attempting to work hard, they invest large amounts of emotional energy in their marriages and end up feeling drained, invariably blaming their partners for depleting them so. As any good marital therapist will tell you, many couples, when they seek intervention, usually begin by saying that they have worked very hard on their marriage. And when further probed, it usually becomes clear that by 'hard work', they usually mean the efforts that have gone into making 'compromises'. As the same marital therapist would tell you if the issue were further discussed, a marriage grows enfeebled when the partners compromise their respective needs and settle for a sub-optimal relationship. Which is why, however hard we work on our marriage, it's not going to get much better if we continue to compromise our legitimate emotional, physical and social needs.

With marriage, as with any other field of endeavour, the trick is 'smart work', not 'hard work'. It is a fact of life that we are trained in most other things except how to be married and how to raise children. These, we are expected to have an instinctive knowledge of, almost as a factory-set default. Which explains why, in contemporary times, we see so many defaulters when it comes to marriage. Like anything else in life, we need to learn about marriage, and to do this, our basic attitudes vis-à-vis marriage will have to change. If marriage is viewed as just one more pleasant (or unpleasant) add-on to our lives, we're obviously going to place it on the back-burner, while we get on with our professional and social lives, hoping that the spouse becomes less of a nuisance in the coming years. In this case, obviously the factory-set defaults (your parents' marital and communication styles) will come into operation and the marriage will become more a test of endurance than anything else.

Another aspect of your mindset that needs to be reviewed at this time is what precisely you plan to do with your marriage when you start working on it. Remember, *the idea is not to 'fix' your partner in such a way that you get out of the marriage precisely what you have always wanted.* Also, marriage is not a battleground where childhood conflicts get played out. Neither is marriage a stage of life where we second-guess our partners and ad-lib our ways through roles we believe we are expected to play. As I see it, a marriage needs to have adequate levels of *love, trust, respect and intimacy,* what I refer to as the four pillars of marriage. The work of marriage, then, is to satisfactorily erect these four pillars, however long it takes. And the smart worker makes sure that the appropriate tools are acquired to ensure that the marriage is configured in a manner that it never loses this focus despite the odd shock or crisis that is bound to visit it from time to time.

This means, we need to equip ourselves with the right tools required to work smart on the marriage. As I see it, all the tools we need are geared towards understanding the sub-conscious dynamics in the marriage, for each of us brings our 'excess baggage' into the relationship, whether we want to admit this or not. To 'debug' and reconfigure our marriage, we need to do the following things:

1. *Define the 'marriage space',* also referred to as the *'We space'* or the *'Us space'.* This refers to creating a private, intimate and inviolable marriage environment where we use rational processes to understand and respond to each other's expectations, without any interference or intervention from parents, friends, work

and others. In the marriage space we can be completely ourselves with each other without fear of being judged adversely. I also sometimes refer to this as creating a *marriage bubble* which is protective of the marriage and which is sacrosanct; only both spouses have the password to enter it. Also, both partners define a template for relating to each other that may be derived from templates that they have seen in other marriages, but which will be exclusive, unique and tailor-made to their requirements. (*See Chapters 7 & 8*)

2. *Define respective 'personal spaces', also referred to as 'I spaces'.* Merely because two people get married does not mean that they cease to be individuals. Each has a distinct identity that does need a personal space for self-expression. Smart work means that the two respective 'I spaces' don't come into conflict with each other, nor do they compromise the 'we space'. (*Chapters 9 & 10*)

3. *Fine-tune sexual and emotional intimacy.* This is critical because these are what differentiate marriage from any other close relationship. (*Chapter 11*)

4. *Strategise how to deal with each other's families.* It's about time we started giving soap opera-makers a run for their money and showing them that the 'saas' (mother-in-law) and 'bahu'

(daughter-in-law) need not be problems to each other or the marriage. Also, we need to learn to respect each other's families without bending over backwards to please them. And we need to do all this by remembering that the strategy we develop is targeted at ensuring that we don't break away from our families, but work at enhancing family togetherness. (*Chapter 12*)

5. *Deal with the 'work space' and what is generally referred to as 'work-life balance'.* Today, work does occupy the forefront of our minds. However, it need not compromise our married lives if we take some time to define the boundaries between our work and our marriages. Both can co-exist in comfort. In fact, each of these two spaces can actually symbiotically benefit the other, if we get it right. (*Chapter 13*)

6. *Manage our social lives.* Friends and socialisation can be a source of great personal enrichment if we learn how not to let them eat into the marriage. (*Chapter 13*)

7. *Fight smart.* Fights happen in all marriages. But we need to know how to analyse them and use them to further our understanding of each other. We also need to develop rational methods of resolving conflict in order that our fights don't result in marital toxicity. (*Chapter 14*)

8. *Enhance our communication with each other.* If we can talk *to* each other rather than *at* each other, listen to each other, signal our needs clearly to our partners, understand and respond to our partner's cues appropriately, and learn how to display affection in mutually comfortable ways, we can reformat our marriage to withstand most external and internal pressures. *(Chapter 15)*

9. *Finally, when, how and from whom do we seek help?* We tend to feel that we have all the answers. In today's complex world, the Internet can provide us with insights to some, though not all, of our issues. However, taking help from a professional in these areas could be beneficial, not to 'fix' your marriage, but to give you insights and help you find some of the solutions you may not be able to readily see. *(Chapter 17)*

If it appears to you that marriage is going to involve more effort than you have bargained for, perish the thought! Marriage is a wonderfully enhancing, enriching, enchanting and uplifting experience. As you and your partner get to know each other and experience the joy of openness, transparency and emotional closeness that only a committed relationship can bring you, you will realise what a wonderful experience marriage can be. However, what we need to remember is that we need to configure our marriage properly if it's going to allow us to experience this joy in the long haul. That's why we need to work smart on our marriage and lay our foundations well, preferably in the very first or early years of the marriage. This way we can ensure that the marital relationship we have entered into with exhilaration and anticipation, gives us everything we want and more. This is what the New Indians are doing all over the country. And this is what makes the New Indian Marriage such an exciting 21st-century phenomenon.

3

The Changing Face of Marriage

Sapna was always wary of getting married for she did not want her carefully constructed life to become unpredictable. She had put a lot of energy into her education despite protests from her father who believed that the sooner she got married, the sooner he could retire and spend more time with his buddies at his local adda. Her parents had a fairly typical Indian middle-class marriage and she always felt her mother, who was an extremely talented singer, had to suppress her own aspirations to look after the needs of her husband and family. Also, because she had no income of her own, her mother had been forced to go along with all of Sapna's father's diktats and demands.

Sapna did not want to end up like her mother. She

made sure she got herself a good education and, much to her father's surprise, found a well-paying job in the HR department of a large mobile phone service-provider. She enjoyed her job, the opportunities for travel it provided and the friends she got to make over a short period of six months. However, since she was now considered eminently marriageable, the proposals started flooding in. Even her mother was putting a lot of pressure on her to 'at least allow a few boys to see' her.

Eventually, Sapna agreed to this, provided she was given the casting vote on choosing the right boy. The whole process traumatised her. The nervous but smirking boys who slyly looked at her body, not her eyes, when they talked to her, the oh-so-sweet but equally tough-looking mothers of the boys, the pompous and garrulous fathers who talked down to her, especially when it came to her job. The only saving grace was that nobody pinched and prodded her or asked to look at her teeth. She could fully empathise with cows at a marketplace waiting to be sold to the highest bidder. She rejected all the proposals, even the ones from the boys settled in the US. Her parents were disheartened for they thought that some of the boys were god-sent alliances and simply could not understand why she kept turning all of them down. She told them that she would get married for their sakes if they so desperately wanted her to, but it would be the ultimate sacrifice on her part. They could not accept this for they believed themselves to be modern parents and had always told everyone in their circle of family and friends that they would never force their children to do anything they did not want to. They concluded she had unrealistic expectations of marriage and took her to see all the elders and friends they could think of, who, they hoped, would drill some sense into this adamant girl's head.

Sapna remained unmoved. They asked her to look for alliances on the Internet if she wanted. She was horrified by that prospect. They even said they would accept any boy, even one from a different community, if she could find one such in her office. She could not. Finally, her panicking parents took her to see a counsellor, thinking she may have a deep-seated trauma that turned her against men and marriage. The counsellor asked Sapna what she expected from marriage. 'Emotional fulfilment, companionship and a mutually respectful relationship with a compatible man,' was her reply. The counsellor asked Sapna how old she was. 'Twenty-one,' was the reply.

WHAT IS MARRIAGE?

Sapna's story is not unique. There are thousands of young girls and boys in middle-class India who are forced into marriage simply because their parents feel they must be married off between the ages of 21 and

23. *'Study hard, get a good job, get married'* seems to be the popular mantra. *'Why not? Didn't we get married at that age? And aren't we doing okay now?'* seems to be the predominant defence when parents are questioned on this. What they do not appreciate is that youngsters today do not see marriage the way their parents did— one more inevitable stage in life. We live in an age when, in some metros at least, single women are adopting children, rejecting the idea of marriage after several unhappy relationships, but giving full vent to their maternal instincts. On their part, men too are reluctant to even consider getting married until their careers are well established, since they've worked out how to be their own housekeepers and don't feel ready to assume the responsibilities of marriage and fatherhood. In other words, marriage is no longer seen as an absolute necessity by a growing number of young urban adults. If they feel that they have not found the right partner, they are perfectly prepared to wait until they do, even if this means running the risk of staying single all their lives.

Two related phenomena need to be examined here: the purpose of marriage and the state of preparedness for marriage.

THE PURPOSE OF MARRIAGE

Sapna's expectations of marriage seem hardly unreasonable. If you ask me, they are pretty moderate and pragmatic. Rohit, a young man I recently talked to, had much higher expectations. 'My wife and I should jointly explore our inner selves and together achieve a meaning to our lives that goes beyond the mundane,' he proclaimed grandly.

Whether marriage can accomplish this purpose or not is moot, but I can see where Sapna and Rohit are coming from and where they want to go. Whether we like it or not, marriage is no longer seen as either a necessity or a sacrament. It is increasingly being perceived as a choice that people make to actually enhance the quality of their adult lives. They do not want a repeat of their parents' marriages, unless the latter demonstrably achieved the objective of mutual enrichment. There are, of course, large numbers of young people who have much more banal expectations of marriage. However, when you talk to them a year or two after they are married or if you look at their behaviour in their marriages, you realise that, even if they have not felt it consciously or stated it in so many words, a lot of their expectations of their partners and of marriage are far from commonplace. They expect a lot—and why not? I agree that some of the expectations may be unrealistic, but the way I see it, 'tis better to have unrealistic expectations than to have none at all.

Put differently, the purpose of marriage today is emotional fulfilment. Marriage is no longer merely a procreational or recreational activity. It is not just an add-on option to a young person's life. It is not merely one more social domain to enter. It is seen as an active and vibrant area of life in which one needs to perform well if one is to have a meaningful existence. Unfortunately, since most people lack the necessary tools to format their marriages to fulfil their expectations, they turn to other domains in their lives—principally the work domain—to do this for them. And when they realise that work can never make them feel completely fulfilled, they retire into their own personal emotional crises.

STATE OF PREPAREDNESS FOR MARRIAGE

If you take everything else out of the equation, it is clear that Sapna was just not ready for marriage. She had certain personal goals to achieve before she felt ready to take on the onus of marriage, for though it can give you a lot, marriage can also be an unforgiving taskmaster if you don't get it right. However, even if she did not consciously have personal goals to achieve, it would still be perfectly appropriate for her to delay her marriage.

At the age of 23, Ragini, a popular RJ, was having an exhilarating life. She lived with two friends in an apartment, had her own car and, by virtue of being extremely gregarious and vivacious, was extremely popular with both men and women. She was having a blast of a life, more so because her parents lived in another city and could breathe down her neck only through the occasional telephone call. She could live with this. She simply did not want to get married just yet. *'Perhaps, in a few years' time,'* was her standard response to her parents' anxious queries. It might seem that she didn't really have any justifiable reason to stay single, but she was simply not ready to get married. And frankly, this is good enough reason not to. *'Get married'* can never be the right answer to the question, *'What next?'*

Chiranjeevi was, unfortunately, not so lucky. He was a serious and hard-working, though not brilliant, bank executive, who was just beginning to enjoy his career after several failed attempts at membership of the Institute of Chartered Accountants. He was 26 and was seriously involved with the People for the Ethical Treatment of Animals and a few NGOs concerned with protecting the environment. However, since his mother had recently undergone bypass surgery, he was emotionally blackmailed by a panic-stricken family to get married so that his wife could relieve his mother of the burden of caring for the family. He succumbed. He said yes to the first girl who was paraded in front of him even though she was hardly 'his type' of girl, because he felt that the whole process of 'seeing a girl' was demeaning to the woman and he did not want to subject more women to this indignity. When I last saw them, they were both plodding along, quite unsuited to each other, but stoic in their approach to the whole business of marriage.

One cannot get married to give one's parents a daughter-in-law, or grandchildren, or whatever. One should get married only when one strongly feels the need for companionship and is ready to give of oneself emotionally. Only then can one seek to configure one's marriage for emotional fulfilment. If one sees marriage as an obligation, obviously one will approach it more with a sense of duty than anything else. Probably the most important reason people generally quote when asked why they agreed to get married is that they did not know how to cope with the pressure of staying single particularly when everyone around was busily getting married. Most single people are afraid of being 'on the shelf'. What they need to remember is that in recent times, the average age at marriage in urban India has gone up—to about 26 for women and 30 for men. Panic, therefore, need never determine when one should get married.

In summary, marriage is seen today as a vehicle of personal fulfilment and not merely something that everyone does, or a legal method of having sex and children. Marriage is a partnership, a contract between two consenting adults who are both in a state of preparedness to make a commitment to facilitating each other's growth and personal development by creating a safe, loving, respectful and trusting space as a joint venture. As we shall see in subsequent chapters, a smart marriage is not about compromise or sacrifice. Nor does it need to be a burdensome enterprise, as long as we understand that some preliminary effort is required and some basics need to be put into place.

LOVE OR ARRANGED MARRIAGE?

It is an undeniable reality that urban India has not quite made up its mind about which form of mate-seeking behaviour should be favoured in the 21st century. The protagonists of 'traditional Indian values' naturally plump for the 'arranged marriage'. On the other hand, younger urbanites seem to favour the alternative. I have a problem referring to it as the 'love marriage' for this implies an absence of love in its arranged counterpart, and as we all know, this is far from being the case. However, I will continue to use the term largely because it so widely used and alternatives like, say, the *do-it-yourself* marriage sound cumbersome.

Given that each region in the country has its own love legend, all variations on the Laila–Majnu theme, it does seem remarkable that modern India took such a long time to get on the 'love bandwagon'. However, a closer look at our lore tells us that, more often than not, these love stories end in tragedy. It appears that there is more romance surrounding unrequited, unfulfilled and unconsummated love than its happily-ever-after counterpart. This may well explain why, for centuries, Indians decided to hedge their bets, play safe and opt for 'arranged love', even if it lacks the verve and dash of romantic legend.

The modern urban Indian though, seems to be more entrepreneurial when it comes to choosing a mate. Young people are falling in love in far larger numbers than ever before and the love marriage is no longer a few-and-far-between sort of phenomenon. More interesting is the fact that such events do not provoke the same degree of hysteria, panic and rage they used to. Elopement is no longer a necessity; today there is a higher probability of parental permission and elders' blessings being obtained.

It seems that the love marriage is in our country to stay. But, since it still is a relatively recent phenomenon, it is surrounded by some myths, resulting in unnecessary confusion and entirely avoidable conflicts. Probably the most wide-spread myth is that *love marriages are better than arranged marriages because you know your partner well even before you get married.* However long the courtship, however intense the love, believe me, it's only when you get married that you actually start getting to know your partner. Needless to say, persons in love marriages do have a head start in relationship-building since some of the foundations have already been laid before the wedding, but surprises are part of all marriages. Being prepared for them is not such a bad idea.

Some couples in love seem to believe that *love marriages are more enduring because they are based on love and compatibility.* All good marriages are based on love and compatibility, and without doubt, love is fundamental in a marriage. But it is only one fundamental. You need trust, respect and intimacy if you want to build the marriage. Those marriages that have endured—whether love or arranged—have done so because the couples worked at them. Ask them.

It is often hoped that *the sex is better in love marriages because the partners are less self-conscious.* Couples in love might like to think so, but this is not necessarily true either, for most urban Indians have not yet completely come to terms with their sexuality. Couples in love marriages may end up having good sex, but it is more likely that this will happen after several false starts. A similar scenario is seen in arranged marriages as well, once the many misconceptions about sex that exist in the partners' minds are sorted out. (*Sex and intimacy issues are discussed in greater detail in Chapter 11.*)

Sometimes, one encounters the fear that *couples in love marriages are more likely to 'stray' from their partners.* The tacit assumption here is that couples who fall in love before getting married are probably more licentious than their arranged-marriage counterparts. So, when the marriage starts to stale a bit, their earlier 'promiscuity' gets re-activated and affairs happen. Nothing could be further from the truth. The choice of having an affair is a conscious one and is certainly not dependent on how you choose your mate. Couples in arranged marriages are equally enthusiastic when it comes to extra-marital relationships.

The more sanctimonious among us tend to feel that *couples in love marriages fight more as a result of which more love marriages end up in divorce than do arranged marriages.* It is true that in recent times more and more urban couples are seeking what amounts to a legal solution to an emotional problem. But this is not because theirs was a love marriage. ·Couples in arranged marriages also fight as hard, and the incidence of divorce in arranged marriages is as high. The reasons for why people are seeking divorce more easily today than ever before are quite complex and linked to changing social norms, but love marriages do not suffer more on this score.

So, which is better—arranged or love marriage? There is no answer to this one, simply because neither is better. Whether you fall in love and get married or whether love comes to you after the wedding, it is the way you work on your marriage that determines how successful it will be.

OWNING THE MARRIAGE

Fathima fell in love with a family friend's son, Abdul, and insisted she would get married only to him, even though he came from a much less affluent background. After some initial protests, their parents eventually acceded and the young couple got married in a relatively low-profile ceremony. They left for Dubai soon after, where Abdul had found himself a decent job, and settled down to an apparently unremarkable married life. They seemed to have their spats, but overall they looked happy to be with each other. Fathima's brother Imran, on the other hand, wanted his parents to choose a bride for him. After a lot of careful screening, they found him the young and pretty Meher, and the nikkah was followed by a grand reception. Within six weeks Imran and Meher's marriage started coming apart. Petty fights ended up in major quarrels. Meher did not adjust very well to Imran's parents and was constantly carping about her mother-in-law's sloppy housekeeping. Imran, even though quite besotted with his wife, was enraged by her practice of discussing all their marital problems, including his premature ejaculation, with her parents, who frequently advised him about the best way to keep her happy.

Soon, matters came to a head after Meher overheard a telephone conversation in which her mother-in-law was lamenting to a friend about Meher's conceit and selfishness. Her parents immediately got in on the act. Relatives from both sides positioned themselves on either side of a thorny fence. Insults were traded, ancestors were abused and ultimatums were issued. Finally, some order was restored when some community elders and a wise old mullah intervened, and after much discussion with both families and some counselling of Imran and Meher, it was decided that the couple would live independently for two years, after which they would come back into the joint family. Soon after this, Imran's parents visited Dubai to spend some time with Fathima and Abdul, and marvelled to her about how well she had adjusted despite the wide differences in social background between her and her husband. At this Fathima broke down and confessed that the two of them had a wonderful life until his family came and joined them in Dubai and started interfering in just about everything they did. She was constantly criticised for her lack of housekeeping capabilities, the two of them were not allowed to go out together even to shop for groceries, she was glared at and told not to waste money every time she rang her parents, and her father-in-law constantly told her not to behave like a rich brat even when she did the most harmless of things. She said that Abdul was supportive of her in private, but could never stand up for her in his parents' presence. Fathima's parents were aghast. They wanted to intervene immediately. She stopped them, saying it was her life and she could handle it. After all, Abdul was on her side and she was confident that they would together work out a solution.

The only essential difference between the love marriage and the arranged marriage is that when two people fall in love and make a conscious choice to get married, they 'own' the marriage. They can't blame it on the parents. In arranged marriages this sense of 'ownership' comes in much later. I am not saying that

Fathima and Abdul will resolve all their problems with ease, but at least they are going in the right direction. When I last heard from them, they were still struggling with issues of interference in their marriage, but they were still determined to make it work. Sadly, Meher and Imran never really owned their marriage. Their respective families were the owners of their marriage. And when families get in on the act, usually a lot of emotions are stirred up and reason often takes the back seat, until some wise elder takes matters into hand. I am hoping that Meher and Imran will understand how important it is to own their marriage and not permit others to enter it, for the line between intervention and interference is always pencil-slim.

I have found that ownership of the marriage is the single-most important factor in predicting its success. And it is not a very difficult thing to do. All the couple needs to do is to have an understanding that all marriages, theirs included, will have issues; that regardless of who or what caused these issues, only the couple can resolve these and nobody else; that they need to work together to resolve their issues; that their parents or the marriage broker is not to blame for the issues; that they should actively resist the temptation of involving family and friends in resolving their issues, for family and friends tend to be emotional and biased, however good their intentions; and if they cannot resolve their issues, they are better off seeking help from an unbiased outsider, say a professional. The only caveat I would offer is in cases where abuse—sexual, physical, verbal or emotional—plays a role in the marriage. In this case, involving others right from the beginning may be required, for abuse (*as is discussed in Chapter 16*) needs to be dealt with using a zero-tolerance approach.

4

The New Indian Marriage

From the previous chapters it would be evident that the rules of marriage are changing in India. And about time too! As we discovered, marriage is not just a state one enters into, but a life domain that needs to be nurtured, so that it may provide us what we are all seeking in life—emotional fulfilment. Put differently, the new Indian marriage is growing into a substantial entity that is far more consciously experienced than it ever used to be.

The fact that divorce rates are on the increase doesn't worry me too much. As said earlier, people are still getting re-married. But the way I see it is that increasing divorce rates are just a part of the early reactions to the phenomenon of liberalisation of the new Indian thought process. After years of suppression, we, as a nation, are suddenly discovering that we have the power of choice. So we make our choices more consciously today. However, some of us, intoxicated by this sense of personal empowerment, tend to go over the top a little. Add to this the fact that our levels of tolerance have decreased over the years, and you find more people taking impulsive decisions that they are hard pressed to reverse.

Uma and Satish were married for one miserable year before they decided, by mutual consent, to seek dissolution of their marriage in the Family Court. The reason for their unhappiness was Satish's discomfort with Uma's obsessive pursuit of her career. He had expected that after they got married, she would scale down her career aspirations and pay more attention to their home, which in recent times served pretty much as a hostel to both of them. He could not get his long-suffering mother to live with them, since they were hardly at home, both busy in the pursuit of their respective careers in the IT industry. Their sex life was virtually non-existent, even from the first month of their marriage. Both were simply too exhausted during the week to even contemplate intimacy. And weekends were usually spent recovering from massive hangovers.

Out of the blue Uma was offered an opportunity to go to Ireland for nine months on work. This would mean a huge jump in earnings as well as a promotion. She accepted immediately, without consulting Satish. He was furious, both at being a non-party to the decision-making process, as well as at the fact that she was going away for such a long period. They fought every day on the phone, e-mail and sms. Many nasty things were said. Her boss, a recent divorcee, planted the idea of separation in Uma's head. Uma liked the idea and proposed to Satish that they take a nine-month break from each other and see if this improved their marriage. 'What marriage?' Satish demanded and suggested they call it quits once and for all. She agreed. The very next day a lawyer was sourced from the Internet, and within a week they submitted a petition for divorce by mutual consent.

Fortunately, getting a divorce by mutual consent in Indian law is not all that simple. You first have to establish that you have been living separately for at least six months, after which you have to wait a further period of six months just in case you change your mind. Little more than a year later, nine months of which Uma spent alone in Ireland and had an opportunity to reflect on her life and aspirations, for she was not as overworked in Ireland as she had been at home, they met at the Family Court. Uma had half a mind to withdraw the petition, but pride prevented her from doing so. Satish too, in the past year, had missed her terribly. He too had half a mind to persuade her to change hers. But since he heard her speak with a faint Irish accent, he concluded there would be no point in attempting a reconciliation with someone who had grown so alien, and held his tongue. The divorce was granted. They met again when they picked up their respective copies of the divorce decree and decided to be civil and have a cup of coffee together. Six months and several litres of coffee later, they decided to get married again. Four years on, they remain married.

This is what I mean when I say the new Indian has low tolerance when it comes to dealing with frustration. Admittedly, Uma and Satish were having a very hard time and their respective personal goals appeared to be discordant. However, if they had gone a little deeper, they may have been able to handle things a little differently. On the flip side, if they had not gone through the process of divorce, they may never have discovered that they really did care for each other. Were they then correct in doing what they did? I don't think there is an answer to that, but the way I see it, the fact that they had a choice (divorce), which had perhaps not been available to their parents, did serve to subtly empower them to exercise their right to choose.

I am not saying that this power should be taken away from people. But we do need to remember that, until we reach a certain level of maturity, we may, in the interim period, exercise our choices indiscriminately and without proper application of mind. But this is only a transient phenomenon, not something we should overly concern ourselves with. Think of it as a correction of a situation. Many of the 'older Indians' would have dearly liked to have divorced their spouses, but could not owing to the social stigma at the time. Today the New Indians can. And sometimes, they may overdo it. But, I believe they are smart enough to realise that they don't always have to.

Coming back to my original point, merely because more divorces are taking place now does not mean that marriage is irrelevant in today's life. What it does mean is that the new Indian marriage has to be structured differently than its older counterpart. You might well ask, '*In what way?*' That is what the rest of this book about. But to just give you a broad overview:

The new Indian marriage . . .

* focuses on emotional fulfilment for both partners, and not merely procreation or recreation.
* is owned by both partners in the marriage and not by anyone else.
* recognises two sets of personal spaces ('I' spaces) in a marriage, but pays due attention to the marriage space ('We' space) as well.
* appreciates that fights, issues and conflicts are inevitable when two individuals engage in a close and intense relationship.
* uses rational processes to manage these fights, issues and conflicts.
* employs a zero-tolerance policy towards abuse—whether physical, verbal, sexual or emotional.

* pays adequate attention to the experience and expression of sexual and emotional intimacy.
* believes that parents and children need their own spaces and that these should rest outside of the marriage space.
* works towards transparent and honest communication styles.
* does not hesitate to seek professional help when things get sticky between the partners or they find it hard to find solutions to their issues.
* understands that divorce is a legitimate option (if the marriage does not work despite the best efforts of both partners), but only the final one.

As you read the following chapters, you will realise that the New Indian Marriage is something that every Indian couple can aspire to. All we need to do is to stand back a bit and take fresh stock of our thoughts, beliefs and ideas, and learn how we can work smart on our marriage. We will also see that the earlier we start doing this (preferably in the first year of marriage), the more fulfilling our marriage will turn out.

5

Who's the Right One?
Choosing Your Partner

The foundations for a good and enduring marriage are best laid even before the wedding takes place. I generally recommend that, *at least some of the effort that goes into wedding planning be set aside for marriage planning*. This way one can ensure that the marriage, which we often tend to take for granted, receives its fair share of attention. While your families are busy planning your wedding, you and your partner can start planning your marriage. The way I see it, to plan a marriage, we need to start right from the beginning, from the way we choose our partners and ascertain compatibility.

Sarita felt devastated. She was engaged to be married and was fairly certain that Arun was not quite the person she wanted to spend the rest of her

life with. On the face of it, she had no reason to feel
so. He was good looking, well educated (he was a
paediatric surgeon), had all the 'right' family values
(believed that family life was most important, wanted
an equal partner in his life and not a doormat, was
very respectful of elders, wanted to have children and
play the role of a 'hands-on' father). All her friends
told her that he was a godsend. Who would not want
to marry a man like that? Her parents were already in
love with Arun, and thought they saw in him the son
they never had.

Arun himself was very happy with the alliance. In
fact, on the day of the engagement he told Sarita that
he loved her, and looked just a tad disappointed when
she didn't respond in kind. Thoughts of love were far
from her mind. She was berating herself for having
agreed to the whole thing. When her parents had first
suggested this alliance to her, she was not averse to
meeting Arun, for his résumé sounded quite
interesting. Academically bright, artistically talented
and good looking.

Their first meeting was quite stilted. He seemed
nice enough, but a little vapid, she thought. She did
not sound enthusiastic when she told her parents that
she needed more time to make a decision. Having
thought about it, she announced that she would like
to meet him several more times before coming to a
conclusion. His family backed off on hearing this,
and decided to call off the process. Surprisingly she

felt quite relieved. Not that she was not ready for marriage. She wanted to get married. She had done her MBA at IIM, Lucknow, and straight out of campus, had joined an international bank. Since she was not a very sociable type of person, she found little time to concentrate on meeting men and pursuing relationships. Now, at the age of 28, she was ready to settle down into companionable matrimony and was perfectly willing to go through an arranged marriage. But her lack of enthusiasm about Arun worried her, and she was quite relieved that she didn't have to think about him anymore.

However, within three months, he was back in her life. He seemed to have liked her at the first meeting, and wasn't able to establish comfort with any of the other girls his parents had shortlisted. He insisted to them that he would like to reopen the possibility of marrying Sarita. So, one day, Arun sent her an e-mail saying he would like to meet her for coffee. They had a few chats over the next few weeks, but she still could not feel any chemistry between them. During this period, he also charmed her family and friends, which made matters worse for Sarita, for she seemed to be under pressure from all sides to acquiesce to this alliance. Finally, because she was not able to come up with any convincing reasons to the contrary, she agreed to marry him. They were engaged in an opulent ceremony that involved almost a thousand guests at a flashily decorated banquet hall in a five-star hotel, an occasion he seemed to thoroughly enjoy, but which grated on her sensibilities.

The day after the engagement she told her parents that she wanted to back off. They were devastated, more because she could not come up with a more convincing reason than a vague sense of disquiet that he was not suited to her. The parents were well-respected in their community and could not bear the ignominy of calling off the wedding. Certainly not now. Initially, they were conciliatory in their approach, even condescending. They told her that everybody had premarital jitters, but she was still recalcitrant. Then her family's tone changed. All manner of pressure was brought to bear on Sarita over the next few weeks. She received no support at all for her discomfiture. She was accused of besmirching the family's reputation, of having no love at all for her parents, of arrogance, of not having respect for family values, and was even asked to leave her job which was taking her away from Indian culture. Her kid sister too tried to persuade her by reminding her that in Indian society, boys could get away with murder, but her reputation would be torn to shreds if she broke off the engagement. She would never find a husband, an argument that Sarita was hard pressed to counter. Finally, when she realised that a particularly disagreeable uncle had been entrusted the task of arranging for a detective agency to trail her, to see whether she had a boyfriend stashed away somewhere, she gave in. Her wary parents advanced the date of the wedding to give her less time to change her mind again, and within a few weeks the wedding took place, with a lot of forced camaraderie and gaiety.

Sarita could still not establish comfort with Arun, even though she realised he was a perfectly likeable person. That was her problem: he was likeable but she could not come to love him. She became quite depressed and neglected her work. She could not bear him to touch her, so their marriage remained unconsummated for over a year. Finally, Arun gave up and approached the Family Court to seek annulment of the marriage on the grounds of non-consummation.

It is not at all uncommon, when it comes to marriage, for people to say yes, even if they are not sure of themselves. Sarita, unfortunately, dug herself into a hole because she said yes, even when she had so many doubts. And when she wanted to back off, nobody in her family even tried to understand what she felt. Perhaps, if they had empathised with her, she may have been more ready to acquiesce. Perhaps not. But the major reason for her depression was that she was not given a chance to correct the mistake she had made by saying 'yes' when she should have said 'no'. The important question here is, was Sarita right in placing so much emphasis on 'chemistry' or the lack of it, rather than all of Arun's likeable qualities when it came to choosing her partner?

Compatibility

The way I see it, the answer to that question is 'Yes'. We tend to believe that compatibility is not such an important phenomenon when it comes to choosing our partner. Nothing could be further from the truth than this. Even if we believe that compatibility is important, since we don't have the adequate tools for making a judgement on so abstract a concept, we tend to use star signs, horoscopes, rating scales that we see in our favourite glossy, and other such methods to assess compatibility. Unfortunately, these are inadequate measures of the 'goodness of fit' between two people. In fact, there are really no valid psychometric methods or personality tests to assess compatibility between two people. There is only one way to determine whether an individual is right for you. Does s/he 'feel' right? The answer to this question has to be 'Yes' in the minds of both partners. Arun felt Sarita was right for him. Had Sarita also felt the same, compatibility would have been established, for compatibility requires mutual comfort. But since she did not, the question of compatibility did not arise. They could have done all sorts of personality tests but still remained inconclusive, for such tests can at best predict what kind of issues the couple will have to deal with, not whether they are right for each other.

If, as I say, 'feeling right' is the best criterion in choosing a mate, does it mean that 'love marriages' are a better option, since the 'feel' factor is predominant when one falls in love?

As Sheila and Peter discovered, this is not necessarily true. They met when both of them were doing a medical transcription course following their graduation. You couldn't really call it love at first sight. There was some mutual attraction, but that was about it. Sheila had just recovered from a messy relationship and not quite ready to start another. Peter had just extricated himself from a relationship with an older woman and was quite ready to look for someone his own age and style. Sheila fitted his bill. They were polar opposites, he being flamboyant, even extravagant, and she, sober and down to earth. He thought she was perfect for him, and would keep him anchored. She thought he was a bit of a charlatan. He pursued her vigorously. Slowly but steadily he wore down her defences. Finally, she relented, and soon realised that she was very much in love with him. They were inseparable and when they finished their course, they both contrived to get jobs in the same company.

He continued to be devoted to her, despite there being several other attractive women in their office who were obviously keen on him. Everything seemed right for them to get married. Both sets of parents were very happy for them to go ahead. However, Peter was filled with a growing sense of discomfort. Sheila had told him that her mother had a drinking problem, from which she had recovered only recently after years of struggle. As a result of this, Sheila had a miserable childhood. Money had been scarce. Her mother had stolen money from home and drank it all away. Instead of feeling sympathy for Sheila when she told him all this, he only felt dread. What if Sheila also turned out like her mother, and turned him into the dispirited and wimpy man her father had become?

He voiced his concern repeatedly to Sheila, who brushed it aside. His misgivings seemed to have some foundations for he noticed that Sheila tended to drink more than necessary at parties, got drunk easily and became irritable with him when she did. She came with him to church only twice during their courtship, even though she knew how important it was to him that they worship together. All his friends told him that she was just a little high-spirited and urged him not to be a wet blanket. Nothing seemed to reassure him, even though he was still very much in love with Sheila. When they made love his doubts seemed to vanish, but they were back again the next day. Soon, he took to confining his doubts to himself for he didn't want to appear like a party-pooper. He dragged on the courtship for as long as he possibly could, using whatever excuses he could find, until Sheila and her family served him a clear ultimatum about setting a date for the wedding. Unable to bear the thought of losing her, and against his better judgement, he agreed, and they got married in a fairy-tale church wedding.

Within two years of marriage Sheila became a full-blown alcoholic. Then followed an endless round of doctors, hospitals, rehab centres and relapses. He couldn't stand more than five years of this. He secretly made plans to emigrate, and escaped to Australia where he currently lives. They are still technically married, but I can't see them making it work, unless Sheila undergoes a miraculous transformation, which though not impossible, has not happened so far.

As Peter discovered, love does not conquer all. Being in love is an enchanted state to be in, but if another part of you is signalling that something's wrong somewhere, you will probably be well advised to pay heed to it. Sarita couldn't and Peter didn't. For this, they paid the price. There will, however be many Saritas and Peters who had suppressed their premarital disquiet, got married and did not suffer the fate that these two did. They were taking a chance, and that things worked out well in the final chapter for them is a bonus that one is truly happy for. However, things could have gone the other way too. Each one of us will have to decide how much of a chance we want to take. But the most important thing is that this should be done consciously. If one has decided that one will indeed take the plunge despite the disquiet, one must do so in a spirit of positivity. Otherwise, the feeling that things are not quite what they should be can grow like a cancer, and later might become the very reason for the relationship to break. It is conceivable that Peter's apprehensions ended up setting in motion a self-fulfilling prophesy.

If one has indecisiveness as a personality trait or if one is waiting for the perfect man or woman, this feeling of disquiet will be possibly experienced every time one 'sees' a man or a woman with matrimony in mind. Unfortunately, this can also cloud the picture. If you find it difficult to make up your mind when faced with any dilemma, the disquiet you experience is just your usual reaction to making a choice. This is not to be confused with what Peter and Sarita experienced. In such a situation, everything else being equal, I would recommend you take the plunge with confidence, for most indecisive people usually become comfortable with the choices they made, however agonising the process was. If your disquiet is on account of the fact that you are searching for the perfect person, abandon the search straightaway, for such a person doesn't really exist. The least imperfect of your suitors should work perfectly well for you. However, if these are not the reasons for your doubt, think really hard and whichever way you decide to go, do so with a bold step and with self-belief. Only then can you make your choice work for you.

To sum it up, when it comes to choosing your partner, your instincts can be very powerful allies. More often than not, your instincts are self-protective mechanisms. I am not suggesting that they will always be right. Sometimes they make us look rather silly and take us in inexplicable directions, but if we give them a regular workout, they slowly get honed. So, if you feel the chemistry is not quite right, listen to your instincts. They're probably telling you that your pheromones are mismatched.

Pheromones are chemical substances secreted by the body that by their odour attract or repel a person of the opposite gender, thereby accounting for the term 'chemistry' in relationships. And some amount of attraction is vital to the success of a marriage. However, also do remember that merely because your pheromones are resoundingly matched, it does not necessarily mean that your relationship is on the fast track to success. If your emotions don't match, you might end up having great sex but a lousy marriage. And the only way you can tell whether you are a good emotional match is by allowing yourself to feel the indefinable X factor in the relationship: to see whether you really feel comfortable enough with your partner with whom you'll probably have to spend the rest of your life. Even if a strong 'feel-good' doesn't exist, it doesn't matter. But if a 'feel-bad' or 'feel-uncomfortable' is in evidence, then please pay attention and explore it before you take your final call. This is true for both arranged as well as love marriages. At this point, let us also be clear that the 'feel-good' element is no guarantee of a wonderful marriage. It just means that the chances of making your marriage a wonderful one are higher.

6

Not Quite There:
Courtship & Engagement

I have, for some time now, been an advocate of a longish engagement period, once the decision to get married has been taken. By longish I mean at least six months for a love marriage and nine to twelve months for an arranged marriage. This engagement period serves a very important role. In an arranged marriage, it works as a preliminary period of courtship where the affianced can, if they utilise the period properly, permit themselves the experience of at least some of the emotions that young lovers usually go through. In a love marriage, now that the commitment issue has been laid to rest, at least in part, the partners can extend whatever feeling states they experienced earlier with less anxiety and more intensity. But more than this, the engagement period helps both partners lay the foundations for the future roles they will be playing as husband and wife. They start seeing themselves not just as a man and a woman, but as two people who are going to embark on a journey which they would enjoy more if they were well prepared. If you've had a short engagement and are already married when you read this, don't worry yourself too much. Most of the things described in the following pages can well be undertaken during the early part of your marriage as well; often the first year or so of married life is not very different from an extended engagement, given the levels of tentativeness with which each partner approaches the other.

Spend time with each other

The first thing you need to do when you're engaged is to negotiate with your respective families to have the opportunity to spend as much time with each other as you possibly can. By and large, most urban families are not entirely unwilling to permit this, unless you belong to a very conservative community, in which case you might want to consider taking the assistance of technology. Telephone conversations, Internet chats (particularly video chats) and so on, while not actually being complete replacements for face-to-face contact, are better than nothing at all. If yours is a love marriage, make sure you consciously make time to spend with each other instead of settling into a complacent belief that you know everything about each other. You will realise that there are still many discoveries that will be made. I am not suggesting that you must get to know every possible thing about each other before tying the knot (this is impossible to achieve), but using this time to create a road map for your marriage is not at all a bad idea.

Saying 'yes' does not mean you've made a complete commitment yet

Most people think that the decision to get married is tantamount to making a complete commitment. Unfortunately, this is not quite true. Agreeing to get married is only the gateway to a commitment. You still have some work to do. Since there will be ups and downs in your marriage you need to make a commitment to work on your marriage regardless of the issues that come up. Also, you need to remember that you are not making a commitment to your partner, you are making a commitment to yourself to stay in the relationship and find creative solutions to even the stickiest of problems, because it is in your own interest to do so. It will make you a more rational problem-solver. This would probably be a good time to examine the basic template for the New Indian Marriage (*described at the end of Chapter 4*) and see how both of you respond to the concept.

Your parents' marriage is not necessarily the best template for yours

The only marriage that most people have observed closely is that of their parents. And invariably, they end up trying to thrust their respective parents' templates down each others' throats. You need to be as objective about your parents' marriage as possible; learn to adopt what works for you and your partner, and reject what does not. If both of you look closely enough at your respective parents' marriages as openly as possible, you might be able to together develop a workable template for your own.

Keep your wedding ceremony down to mutually agreed basics

More often than not, the first signs of schism that appear in a marriage start at the wedding ceremony itself, as we will discuss a little later. As a simple rule of thumb, the more elaborate the ceremonial rituals, the more the chances of treading on somebody's corns. And once matters reach the level of an ego tussle, a bad taste is often left in everyone's mouths. A good idea would be for both of you to agree on the kind of ceremony you want and be involved to the extent possible in ensuring things go the way you planned. If you're unable to do this, at least resolve not to hold each other responsible if there are any unpleasant incidents, since, as any event manager will tell you, glitches always happen when organising large-scale events. And it's no one person's fault really, except, possibly, the wedding planner's.

Plan your financial future together

I know that it can be awkward to talk money when you have wine, roses and sex on your mind. However it would be a prudent investment of time if both of you can talk about your financial future. Gone are the days when the man was the provider-protector and the woman the homemaker. Today both genders share both roles equally, and each partner would expect to know how the family finances are to be managed. If you do this even before you get married, it makes your future easier.

Talk sex

In the unlikely event that you have not yet had any form of sexual contact with each other, the engagement period may be a good time to talk and explore your respective sexual attitudes and anxieties with each other. Most couples therapists will tell you that, in both love and arranged marriages, the commonest problems during the first year are related to sex and sexuality. Remember that your partner is as anxious about the whole sex thing as you are, and instead of struggling with each other's fears and anxieties on the *suhaag raat*, you might be well advised to have this conversation much earlier. As a corollary, it might be well worth remembering that few marriages get consummated on the wedding night any more; most partners sleep through it.

Don't expect your partner to love your family like you do

Here's the bottom line: You love your mother, your father and your siblings because they are your mother, father and siblings. Expecting your partner to love them like you do is one of the major causes of early marital problems, particularly since it's unlikely that you are going to love your partner's family the way she/he does. If both of you are able to talk frankly to each other about your respective family members, you can start off married life with the reasonable expectation that you don't get stuck at that most basic of all marital conflicts: 'Me and my family vs. You and your family'.

Work out a balance between work and your partner

I know many young people who continue to give priority to their work even after they are engaged. The partner, naturally, perceives this as a harbinger of things to come and starts off married life on a note of disappointment than one of positive expectation. If this is the case, your marriage is more likely to have difficulties, than not. So, even as you cater to your team leader's demands, try and spare a thought for your poor betrothed, whose birthday has completely slipped your mind. And try not to come up with the excuse that birthdays aren't important to you, when yours actually is. If you do, you condemn yourself to a lifetime of no birthday parties.

Your friends, my friends, our friends

Friends are a very important part of one's life. But do remember that your partner too has friends and that s/he may not like all your friends. This does not mean that you've therefore got to abandon your friends. Far from it. Together, you can expand your network of friends and even make new ones, provided both of you are open to this possibility.

Try and listen to each other

Listening, unfortunately, is something that most of us don't do very well. Invariably we wait, either politely or impolitely depending on the kind of person we are, for the other person to finish what they are saying, so we can get back to hearing our own voice. Sometimes we don't even bother waiting. We just cut in. We can do better than this. Actually we need to do better than this. Only by listening to what our partner is trying to say, can we really get a proper feel of the person. However, please do remember that being a good listener alone is not enough. One has to express oneself clearly too.

Clarify expectations of each other

It would be useful to admit that we all have expectations of our partners. I know many people who grandly proclaim, 'I have no expectations of my partner; therefore I want my partner also not to have any expectations of me', completely oblivious to the fact that expecting the partner not to have any expectations is an expectation in itself. Since marriage is a purposeful relationship, you are bound to have expectations of your partner. If you spent some time trying to understand what these are, you will be in a better position to articulate them to your partner. Articulation is absolutely necessary; expecting your partner to anticipate your expectations and respond proactively to them is probably the most irrational thing you can do. Nobody can read your mind, not even yourself. When you have identified what your expectations are, don't be afraid of stating them clearly.

However, also provide for the fact that your partner may not be in a position to—or may not even want to—fulfil all your expectations in one go. It is conceivable that your partner may find some of your expectations irrational. If this is the case, try and examine whether there is any truth to this. If you honestly feel there isn't, then stand your ground and learn to agree to disagree with your partner. Also, don't push your partner too much to acquiesce, for doing so may actually put unnecessary pressure on the process of communication. Remember, the object of communication is not agreement. You don't have to convince your partner of the correctness of your position. You merely have to express what you feel strongly about. As long as you learn to stand your ground, even while being open to the possibility that your stand may be wrong, you will be able to establish a greater degree of harmonious communication later in your marriage.

7

The 'We' Space

Venkat and Chitra met each other on a matrimonial website. They entered into a long and engaging e-correspondence that both thoroughly enjoyed. Their appeared to be a goodness-of-fit between both of them and they finally decided to meet in person. He was delighted to have found a girl who was as close to her family as he was to his and she felt highly reassured that he wanted a working wife, not to augment the family finances, but because he believed in women's economic independence. Their comfort with each other grew even more when they met for a face-to-face chat. The discovery that their respective fathers had their roots in the same village was an unexpected bonus.

In a few months, they got married and she shifted to his family home. There were no major adjustment issues with her in-laws, since they led a similar lifestyle to the one she was accustomed. Soon, she got into a routine. Wake up, go the gym for a workout, make her bed, clean her room, have breakfast, go to work, go to her parents' house when she finished work, wait for Venkat to pick her up on his way back home, eat dinner at her parents' if Venkat got delayed or go back to his home for dinner if he came home early, make love if both were up to it and then go to sleep. On Friday evenings, she went to the temple and on Tuesday evenings visited her mother's parents, as she had done for several years. On Saturdays, after she came back from work (she worked half a day on Saturdays), she had a nap, then got ready for the evening's revelries with Venkat's friends at some pub, nightclub or friend's house. She didn't particularly enjoy this but she went along in the spirit of mutual adjustment, for he seemed to enjoy it. On Sundays, both of them slept most of the day to recover from the exhaustion of the previous week and to recharge themselves for the week to come. She was not uncomfortable with Venkat's parents, though she was not particularly close to them either. She was perfectly happy with her life, she felt.

But Venkat was not. He felt Chitra was not really engaging with his family, nor was she taking any part in the running of the household. Neither was he, but he never had, so he didn't find this peculiar. But he felt she was treating his home like a hostel. And he didn't like this. Although there was a lot of passion in their sex life, he didn't really miss her when she was not around. His diagnosis was that Chitra was not doing anything special for him to make him dependent on her, so he came up with the idea that they should move from his parents' home and set up an establishment of their own. She wasn't too crazy about the idea, because she felt that things were fine as they were. But after a few tantrums on his part, she acquiesced. His parents were perfectly amenable to this, although her parents voiced considerable trepidation. Venkat held his ground and soon they moved to a small apartment near her parents' home. Because neither of them could cook, they engaged a cook whom they had to sack when she, taking advantage of their absence, was found entertaining strange men in their apartment. They couldn't find an adequate replacement, so they started depending on nearby eateries and takeaways. They had to abandon this when Chitra came down with a painful attack of amoebic dysentery that required hospitalisation. After this, they started getting their meals from her parents' kitchen in tiffin carriers. Other than this, her routine continued as it used to be. So did his.

When you don't actively define the marriage space, both of you will continue to function in your own independent spaces and while there may not be too much friction as in Chitra's and Venkat's marriage, there is not going to be a whole lot of joy and communication either. Neither Venkat's nor Chitra's lives changed significantly after they got married. Save for the fact that they now had sex regularly, their pre-marital lives were remarkably similar to their married lives. Both their routines remained the same. I have no idea how long they will continue in this state of ennui. Many couples do choose to have this kind of marriage, preferring it over a friction-ridden type of relationship. But rarely does this pattern last. Usually, an external event such as a job transfer or the death of one of the parents or some equally traumatic crisis comes along and turns the marriage inside out. Unfortunately, since they have not built a marriage space, they are poorly equipped to handle such storms.

Another kind of scenario is also very common in our country. Since we exist in a patriarchal system, it is customary for the wife to move into the husband's family home. In this situation, the young bride is often expected to fit into the lifestyle and rituals of her new home. While on the surface this may not be very difficult to do, it can seem overwhelming to a new bride if she suddenly moves into a large joint family and starts off as the general dogsbody. The adjustment is even more difficult if the girl has led an easy life in her parents' home or if she has lived in a nuclear family. In this case, the girl will be 'broken in' by her new in-laws and most of her conscious preoccupation will be on how to deal with her husband's family. The husband, on his part, has little idea of what is happening at home unless his wife tells him. Even if she does tell him, he does not know how to deal with this situation and ends up either avoiding it all together or making a scene with his family members, thereby putting her in a position of even greater disadvantage. In this case the only marriage space they have is in their bedroom, where she is not permitted, by virtue of her allocated household chores, to spend too much time. And more often than not, their primary communication is through sex or when they go out to an occasional movie or to dinner, neither environment necessarily conducive to a good heart-to-heart.

Often, in the early stages of marriage, young brides are asked to concentrate on establishing a good relationship with the parents-in-law in the expectation that once this peak has been conquered, the rest will be smooth-climbing. Maitreyi did just this, as she was advised to by her mother, and together mother and daughter invested a lot of time in working out strategies that she could employ to win her mother-in-law over. As it turned out, her efforts paid off, for soon her mother-in-law was completely on her side, much to her father-in-law's chagrin, for he had spent most of his corporate life using a divide-and-rule strategy and found himself increasingly alienated from his own wife, who seemed more keen on seeking her daughter-in-law's opinion than his own. He couldn't be angry with Maitreyi, though, because she was most attentive to his needs too and was well on the way to earning herself the sobriquet of 'perfect daughter-in-law'.

It was not that she was manipulative or scheming. Maitreyi genuinely believed that if she invested time and energy on her parents-in-law, she could have a great marriage. During this period, probably the only thing she did for her husband, Ajay, was to 'give him sex' regularly and to her eyes, he looked quite happy about the whole thing. However, after a few months she realised that her husband was spending more time at work than he used to, having late-night telephone conversations that he'd hastily terminate when she entered the room, refusing to let her touch his mobile phone and generally becoming distant from her. It turned out that he was having a crisis at work and not having anyone to talk to, was spending a lot of time with a female friend, on whom he was progressively becoming more dependent.

Fortunately, the situation was salvaged, for nothing of any consequence had really taken place. But it could have gone either way. Many variations of the above scenarios can be seen in Indian marriages and I have seen far too many couples struggling to lay the foundations for a successful married life at a later time in the marriage, when this is probably among the first things they should have done.

WHY IS IT SO HARD TO DEFINE
THE MARRIAGE SPACE?

Before we get into the elements that need to be considered while defining the marriage space, let us first look at a few issues that may come in the way of doing so.

Is marriage space necessary?

First off, both of you need to be convinced that your marriage needs space to grow into something more fulfilling. Leaving aside fulfilment for the time being, even to perform its basic functions, a marriage needs space. Only when you define your marriage space do you facilitate the process of bonding with your partner, and it is the strength of this bond that is going to see both of you through the rest of your lives. I know that in our country, space is not considered such a big deal. We tend to get by in overcrowded environments. And when I talk about space, many people tend to say that they have a bedroom of their own. Needless to say, that's not the kind of space I am talking about. Not surprisingly, men tend to ask more often whether space is really necessary. Women seen to have an intuitive understanding, regardless of their social background, that marriage space is important. Of course, they may not refer to is as 'space'. They use a variety of terms to describe the marriage space: closeness, spending time, privacy and so forth.

Marriage space is all of these, but it is also much more. To my mind, marriage space exists inside your head and is hardly defined by the geographical space you have at your disposal. *It is not what you do but the comfort with which you do it* that determines how much space you have allocated to marriage in your life. In the final analysis, marriage space gets defined by how much you value your marriage and your partner, how much priority you are willing to accord to your marriage and your partner, how much time you are willing to allocate to nurture your partner, how much you permit your partner to nurture you, how much you own your marriage and how much of yourself you are willing to share with your partner. All these create and strengthen the bond between both partners. So, you see, marriage space is all about the attitude you have towards your marriage, your partner and the bond between both of you. And surely you'd agree with me that both of you need to have similar attitudes and approach to the marriage?

Is marriage a priority in our lives?

Varun always insisted that when he came home from work, he liked spending time with his parents and kid sister, having dinner with them, maybe watching a bit of TV with them, as he had always done. After this he was happy to spend time with Anamika, his wife. But she was never happy, always wanting more of his time and attention. On further exploration, it transpired that Varun woke up around eight in the morning, rushed to work around nine, came home at around nine or so in the evening, showered, had dinner and watched television with his family till about 11, checked his mail and surfed the Internet till about 11.30 and then wanted to chat with Anamika. Since she had to get up around 6 in the morning to attend to domestic chores before she left for work, she was exhausted by 11.30 and could barely manage to stay awake till midnight. Some desultory conversation would ensue, maybe some sex which she was waiting to get over with, and both would fall asleep in seconds. There are, of course, other couples who have more time than Varun and Anamika with each other. But often, the time spent together is not necessarily quality time, for technology—the mobile phone (calls from office, friends and others), television or the computer— constantly intrudes.

So, to define your marriage space, you have to learn to prioritise each other and the marriage over other issues. By this I don't mean you give up everything else in life, lock yourself in a room and stare into each others' eyes. By all means do all the things you want to, but make sure you give your marriage and your partner your full attention and energy and enough time. Doing this may mean rearranging your schedule a bit, but that shouldn't be such a big deal, should it? It was only when Anamika drew up a spreadsheet that she was able to get Varun to appreciate how little time and energy he had for the marriage. They worked out a revised schedule whereby Varun stopped watching TV with his family, but increased the time he spent at dinner with them instead of rushing through the meal, and after dinner he and Anamika went for a walk in their colony, chatted and bonded with each other.

Another reason that young men are reluctant to be seen to be giving time to their partners is the worry that their family members and friends will feel that they are neglecting them. So they feel the need to establish parity between wife, parents, siblings and friends, even if they feel the need to spend more time with the wife. This is a cultural phenomenon in our country and generally, young husbands tend to be mercilessly and sometimes maliciously ragged about this by parents, siblings and friends. Everybody seems to have the unstated fear that the new bride is going to 'take away' the son/brother/friend unless something is done about it, and everyone has their own vested interest in delaying the definition of the marriage space.

Strangely enough, this phenomenon does not apply to the wife. She is expected to forsake everything else for the sake of the husband and the marriage. Come on, guys! Surely putting your wife first is not going to make you a *joroo ka gulam*? As long as you deal with this in good humour, and don't get too worked up about it, and reassure everybody else in your environment that it is most natural to want to spend quality time with your wife, you should be able to get through this stage. Remember, it is your wife who's going to be around for the rest of your life. Some initial investment in her and the marriage should certainly be worth your while.

Resistance to change

I have lost count of the number of people who start off their married lives by saying, 'Don't ever attempt to change me.' I understand what they mean by this. There is often a fear that marriage threatens one's individual identity and therefore one feels the need to stoutly resist any attempt by the spouse to change one's behaviour. As a result of this apprehension, even if the spouse says something constructive, one tends to dig one's heels in and refuse to respond.

Kumar was actually a non-smoker. However, whenever he started dating a girl, he started smoking. The day she asked him to stop smoking, he would dump her, for he believed she was encroaching on his individual rights and personal liberties. He felt this was the acid test of whether or not a girl wanted to change him and was generally quite pleased that he had discovered a formula for assessing compatibility. Several girls came and went and he finally met Vinita who was a heavy smoker herself. Since she never asked him to stop smoking, he married her. Today, he is the one who's after her to quit the habit so they can have children.

We need to acknowledge the fact that, as growing human beings, we are all subject to changes in our ideas, attitudes and beliefs. It would be foolhardy to resist change, for change is inevitable and will take place whether you want it or not. In fact, the more we resist it, the more we cramp our personal growth. Don't we all read self-help books and attend expensive inspirational workshops that promise us that our lives will change forever? So what is wrong, pray tell me, in listening to constructive suggestions coming from our spouse? While I do agree that our partner may lack the experience or the credibility of a Covey or a Khera, it is our partner who knows us and understands us the best. Even if some of our partner's exhortations may come from a position of personal prejudice—as for example when one of the partners in a marriage overreacts to a father's alcoholism by demanding that the other not even engage in occasional social drinking at office parties—not all such suggestions come from irrational spaces.

Furthermore, if you work on configuring your marriage appropriately, you will find that these irrational spaces slowly recede and eventually disappear. I am not suggesting you go along with all of your partner's irrational requirements. We need to have (*as we will discuss in Chapters 9 and 10*) a way of defining boundaries in the relationship that keeps our respective identities intact. But, we also need to remember that marriage is certainly going to change us. If we are smart we will make it change us for the better.

'I don't need anybody'

In recent times, perhaps because of the insecure environment we all live in or perhaps because we have been in a couple of relationships that we ended up getting hurt in, we tend to fear getting dependent on our partner, in the belief that we expose ourselves to vulnerability. This is perfectly true. We are vulnerable when we are dependent. Unfortunately, there is no way we can have a relationship without becoming dependent on our partners. Dependency is the very cornerstone of a relationship, and without it, relationships cannot become deep. In the absence of depth, a relationship cannot give us the joy and emotional fulfilment we are looking for. This is because dependency is an intrinsic human need. We all have a need to love and be loved. And when we look for somebody to love us, we immediately become vulnerable, for we depend on them to love us to make us feel complete.

We are also vulnerable because we see ourselves through the eyes of the one we are dependent on. If they have a negative view of us, we end up feeling negative as well. When we do not receive affirmation from the one we are dependent on, we feel unhappy and wretched. What is the way out of this vulnerable position? Do we build a wall around ourselves, deny ourselves our need for dependence, and thereby remain invulnerable?

Deepa was madly in love with Vikram right through their medical college days. He was the class all-rounder, sportsman, champion debater and, far and away, the best looking guy in college (every class has one of these guys, much to the chagrin of all the other boys). Naturally, he was much sought after by all the girls in the college, but he seemed to like her more than the others. She couldn't quite understand why for there were far prettier girls in college, but she was grateful nevertheless. Their relationship endured and in course of time, after they completed their post-graduate training in paediatrics, they got married.

She wanted to become a surgeon, but because he chose paediatrics, so did she. She worked hard to make sure that all of his needs were met. She believed it was her duty to look after him and spent most of her energy on coming up with different ways of pleasing him. She cringed every time he was nasty to her, which was happening with greater frequency because she was a better paediatrician than he was. Realising this, she slowly reduced her medical practice and eventually gave it up altogether after their first child was born. He seemed happy when she did this.

He was never very loving to her, although he was not hostile either. She slowly cut herself off from her family, since Vikram never really liked them. Any scraps of love that came her way, she accepted gratefully. When she saw him looking at other women, she immediately increased her exercise routine, went to the beauty parlour and bought herself a new set of clothes, to seduce him back. He never seemed to appreciate all she did for him. Even though he was perfectly happy with their sex life because she indulged all his fantasies, she had never had an orgasm, except when she masturbated, which she had recently started to do. Even though she was unhappy, she never complained too much, since she was terrified that he would divorce her, as he threatened to every time they fought.

If you look closely at Deepa's story, three things stand out. One is that she was over-dependent on Vikram for her wellbeing, second is that she had 'doormatted' herself as a result of which she had no life of her own and no personal space, and third is that the dependency equation in the relationship was quite lop-sided in that she was more dependent on Vikram than he was on her. In this kind of a situation, anyone is bound to experience a great sense of vulnerability and insecurity for one is never really sure of one's partner. However, this need not be the way things should be in all relationships.

It becomes clear that for comfortable dependence

without vulnerability to exist in a relationship, two parameters have to be put in place: Mutual dependence (or inter-dependence) and personal spaces. When both partners are mutually dependent on each other, both are equally vulnerable, or looked at differently, equally invulnerable. For this to happen, each must have their own personal spaces which they can luxuriate in so they are not over-dependent for affirmation only on each other. Rarely is inter-dependence perfectly mutual, for at different stages of life, one partner will be slightly more dependent than the other. This is perfectly normal, as long as both partners have a clear understanding of this phenomenon, are able to provide adequate reassurance to the dependent partner, and do not permit things to become as lop-sided as they did in Deepa's and Vikram's relationship.

DEFINING THE MARRIAGE SPACE

Now that you have understood the need for the marriage space, you can get down to the actual task of defining it. What you're going to now read is not an exercise that you complete in one sitting. It involves several conversations and you may actually get down to it when an event happens in your marriage that pushes your thinking in this direction. What you need to do is to create a conducive environment for your marriage space to be defined in the first year of your marriage. To do this, you need to make sure that none of the obstacles to defining marriage space exist.

To recap, you need to:

- prioritise your marriage
- create time for your marriage
- be amenable to change
- and not be afraid of dependence on your partner.

If you have done all of this, you'll find that defining your marriage space is something that will happen at a comfortable pace as the two of you start getting to know each other better.

Clarifying each partner's expectations of the other

The first area you need to explore is the expectations you have of your partner's and your role in the marriage. How do our expectations form? Usually, during our adolescence and later, during young adulthood, we start having certain ideas about what we expect from our spouse. If we have had a couple of relationships, we learn from some of the mistakes we committed in these. Or we may learn from the relationships of some of our close friends, cousins or other family members. We also tend to learn from movies, books and television.

Some of us may have thought about these matters consciously and have very fixed ideas. Others may have only a vague notion. Sometimes, we have role models and therefore want our marriage to be like theirs—even if we have very little idea of what actually happens in their marriage. I remember one young man who wanted his marriage to be like Sachin Tendulkar's, so he wanted to marry a doctor, even though, when probed deeper, he had no idea what kind of marriage the cricket icon had. In other words, when we get married, we do have some conscious expectations of our partners that may or may not be fully formed and clear. And these expectations vary tremendously across individuals, determined largely by personal experiences and sub-cultural factors.

The only expectation that I have seen as unvarying across subcultures and personal experiences in our country is the expectation stated by the average Indian male that his mother is the most important person in his life and that his wife should not only accept this, but also feel the same way. Hardly a promising basis to start off married life, one would imagine! We will be dealing with parents in a subsequent chapter, so I won't comment on this universal Indian expectation just yet, except to say that it is pretty unrealistic to expect your partner to develop the same emotional intensity for your parents as you.

Expressing our conscious expectations of each other is usually not very difficult. But we must try and state these as concretely as possible, so there is no ambiguity at all in the way we expect our partner to respond. For instance, there is no point stating that you want your partner to be your friend. To different people, 'friend' means different things. So, you need to state this more clearly. For example, 'I want you to listen to me when I talk to you about my work', 'I would like you to cheer me up when I'm feeling down by saying or doing something funny' and so on. When you state your expectations, don't ask your spouse to treat you the way your ex did or the way another friend does. Nobody likes to be compared (I'm sure neither do you).

Probably the most important aspect of clarifying your expectations with your partner is adhering to the *four golden rules of clarifying expectations.*

First golden rule:

Just because you have stated your expectation does not mean that your partner HAS to comply with it.

It is important that you clearly state your expectation, but it is equally important to appreciate that your partner may not be ready to respond to it just then. Maybe your partner may find the expectation irrational. This does not necessarily make you an irrational person. It just means that your partner doesn't know you well enough just yet to respond positively to your expectation and therefore considers it irrational.

Ajit, an occasional drinker, considered Pooja's insistence that he not touch a drop of alcohol irrational. He understood that it came from her own traumatic experience of her brother's unhappy relationship with alcohol, but in his line of business, he had to entertain clients and could not function as a teetotaller. He did not want to do anything behind her back and insisted that while he would not drink recreationally, he would have a drink or two when he entertained. To put it differently, *as much as you have a right to state your expectations clearly, your partner has an equal right to defer complying with them.* If you approach this whole process rationally, you'll find that you don't fight about it, but genuinely try and understand your partner's personality through the expectations that are presented. There may be some expectations you may never be able to comply with, but if you follow the second golden rule, your partner will appreciate that you are approaching the whole process positively.

Second golden rule:

Even if you feel that your partner's expectation of you is irrational, do not pass adverse judgement on your partner, but try your best to respond to it without breaking your back and, if despite your best efforts you are unable to, clearly state that you are not able to do so.

When you approach this on a best-effort basis, you will find that your partner, appreciative of your efforts, may even give up the expectation altogether.

As Pooja and Ajit's relationship grew more comfortable she realised he was keeping his promise about alcohol. She started relaxing and stopped coming in the way of recreational drinking, even occasionally joining him in a glass of wine. Another time Pooja appreciated the second golden rule was when she tried her best to respond to Ajit's need that she wake up at 5 A.M. and join him in his workout, although she was used to going to the gym in the evening after work, so she could wake up a little later in the morning. Seeing how this interfered with her energy levels during the day, Ajit, grateful that she did try, suggested she go back to her old routine. Actually, it didn't really matter whether they worked out together or not, but because she was not judgemental about his expectation, and she made a genuine effort, this made him feel good. Also this made him more amenable to responding to her expectation that he switch off his mobile phone for at least an hour every evening when they were together.

Our conscious expectations are not much of a problem, but becoming aware of your unconscious or hidden expectations of your partner is a little more tricky. There is one way in which you can have an indirect indication of them. You can look at the way you treat your partner. Often, what we display to others is what we want them to do for us. For instance, if you take a lot of trouble over your partner's birthday and go out of your way to ensure that it goes off perfectly, chances are that you want your partner to make a similar fuss over you on your birthday.

You may find that your partner, not being a 'birthday fuss' sort of person, may not have expected you to have taken the trouble, and is therefore not likely to do so when your birthday comes along. This brings us to the third golden rule.

Third golden rule:

Just because you have certain ways of behaving in certain situations, don't expect your partner to do the same.

However, if you recognise your behaviour as reflecting your own needs and give your partner a clear indication that this is the way you'd like to be treated on your birthday, then you will be observing the fourth golden rule and may end up not being disappointed.

Fourth golden rule:

Don't expect your partner to instinctively know what you want. State what you want clearly.

If your partner is sensitive enough and is able to clearly identify your expectations, based on your behaviour, even without your clearly articulating them, treat this as a bit of a bonus, for though this does happen, it is not a common occurrence.

Once you have clarified your expectations of each other, both partners generally feel a little easier with each other. This is mainly because of the feeling that each has become more predictable to the other. A basic communication platform for the marriage space has been created and both partners are now ready to examine the kind of marriage templates they would like to base their future relationship on.

8

'Good' Wives & Husbands: Marriage Templates

From clarifying your expectations of each other, you may have a fair idea of what kind of marriage template both of you want for yourselves, but before you freeze on this, there is one more thing you should do. You need to understand the template that exists in your subconscious mind and that you have entered the marriage with, even though you may not even know it's there. A marriage template is nothing but the way you think a marriage should be conducted: the way you will behave with your partner, the way you expect your partner to behave with you. In other words, how each of you defines a good wife and a good husband.

Typically, the marriage that we have viewed closely is that of our parents, or older relatives, or friends, whoever we were closest to. Even if we don't realise it, each of us has a *role model marriage* imprinted in our subconscious minds. Nine times out of ten, this turns out to be our parents' marriage. As adults, we may have consciously rejected our parents' marriage as not a good enough basis to model our own marriage on. However, whatever we observed as children stays in our minds. And when we face an unfamiliar situation in our marriage, or we are stressed by life events around us, we respond to the situation in the same manner our parents did. It is also possible that we believe that our parents had a wonderful marriage and therefore we have consciously decided that the way they conducted their married life is the way we should too.

PRIMARY AND FINAL MARRIAGE TEMPLATES

The template we have acquired before we get married is called the *primary marriage template* and if both partners have similar primary marriage templates, which does occasionally happen, this makes things extraordinarily easy indeed. (In fact, this is why arranged marriages of yesteryears were based on finding alliances from similar backgrounds, resulting in more or less similar primary marriage templates that required the least adjustment from both partners.) So, we have to get on with the task of defining our *final marriage templates* more consciously than our forefathers had to.

To define the final marriage template, each partner has to explore and share with the other, how they have understood their respective parents' marriage. There is no need to discuss this with the parents to get their clarifications on the finer details (they are hardly likely to share intimate details with you, anyway), because accuracy is not the issue here. *It is your perception of your parents' marriage that determines how you have internalised your primary marriage template.*

For instance, Anita saw her father supportive of her mother's homemaking responsibilities by buying all the groceries, helping with the washing up of the dishes and even sweeping and swabbing the house when the domestic help did not turn up. And she concluded that her father was a very sensitive and supportive man. Therefore, her marriage template expected Nikhil to be of the same mould. How was she to know that the same sensitive father was sexually very demanding of his wife, insisting on sexual gratification even if his wife was exhausted or unwell, without being particularly caring of her sexual satisfaction? Which is why I said accuracy of assessment is not really relevant; whatever has stayed in your mind is what we need to focus on.

A word here on persons whose parents are divorced. It is a common fallacy to assume that because two people divorced each other, their marriage was a failure and therefore had nothing to offer to their children. Not true at all. If you come from a divorced background and you search your memory stores, you will realise that, even though your parents were unhappy with each other, they still did a lot of things that all married couples should do. And whether you like it or not, you have internalised a lot of what they did into your own primary template. As an adult, you can look at their marriage a little more discerningly and try and understand what positives you can take from it.

YOUR OPTIMAL MARRIAGE TEMPLATE

What we all need to shoot for is an optimal final marriage template that works for both partners. Obviously, each partner has their idealised image of perfect wife or perfect husband and when you initially start the exercise, you'll find that you are relating to this idealised image, and not necessarily what your partner is capable of doing for you. But, as you keep talking to each other about your respective primary templates, your partner will be able to point out to you what is doable and what isn't. When both of you discuss your primary templates and get down to defining your final template, the following are the parameters you need to keep in mind:

1) Activities of Daily Living
   a) Live with parents or set up independent establishment?
   b) Homemaking role. Who takes primary

responsibility (need not be a default decision—remember some men have excellent homemaking capabilities)? What is meant by primary responsibility (who has the final say)?

c) Household chores. Who does what? Egs: cooking, cleaning, paying the electricity bill, supervising domestic help, walking the dog.

d) Monthly household budget. Who manages it? What are the sources of funds?

e) Any other activities of daily living that require division of responsibility.

2) Work and finance management

a) Do both work?

b) If it comes to a crunch, whose job will take priority?

c) Working late—how can this be managed?

d) How much of travelling can the marriage handle?

e) How much does each earn? (This is very important; all too commonly, husbands and wives insist on keeping this from each other, resulting in a low-transparency relationship).

f) What kind of bank accounts? One joint account? Two separate bank accounts? One joint and two separate accounts (two 'I' spaces and one 'we' space)?

g) Long-term finance management and savings. Who takes primary responsibility for this (who's better at it?)?

3) Dreams and goals

a) What are his and her dreams for the future—owning a house or several houses, retiring at 40 and travelling the world, having eight children?

b) Attitude toward material acquisitions.

4) Dealing with respective parents and families

a) Whose parents are to be prioritised—his or hers or both?

b) Do our parents sometimes behave irrationally (all parents do, every now and again)? How to deal with parents' irrationalities (*more of this is discussed in Chapter 12*)?

c) How much to extend ourselves for grandparents, siblings and their families? Cousins and their families? What each expects the other to do to accommodate demands made by extended family members?

5) Dealing with friends

a) Large or small social networks?

b) Intense relationships or casual relationships?

c) How close can one get to friends?

d) Attitude to opposite-gender friends—

permissible or problematic? How far and no further?

6) Recreation
   a) Necessary or not?
   b) Movies, bowling, coffee, dinner, pubs, nightclubs, walks by the sea or river, window shopping?
   c) Who decides on weekend plans?
   d) What kinds of weekend plans are acceptable?
   e) Vacations? How many vacations in a year? Romantic or sight-seeing? With others or just the two of you?
   f) Who makes the vacation plans?
   g) Any other joint activities both can undertake (e.g. learning the salsa or whatever).

7) Expression of love to each other
   a) Is it necessary at all or do both assume love for each other and chug along?
   b) Non-sexual hugging, kissing and cuddling in private—acceptable or not? In public? How much is too much?
   c) Birthdays and anniversaries—events to celebrate, or just another day?
   d) Sweet nothings? In person, by e-mail, by sms, or not at all?
   e) Gifts without any reason or occasion?

8) Sex and intimacy (*more of this in Chapter 11*)
   a) How often is good? How much is too much?
   b) What does each want the other to do to enhance the experience?
   c) Sexual variations—are they acceptable or perverse?
   d) If sex is not happening, how to deal with it?
   e) How honest and transparent can we be with each other? Tell each other everything? Or hold back some important stuff? What kind of stuff?
   f) Call each other by name or use an honorific? Special terms of endearment? Only in private?
   g) Horsing around and playing with each other like children—acceptable or horrifying?
9) Health
   a) How healthy do we want to be?
   b) Do we eat to live or live to eat?
   c) Physical exercise—yes, no, how much?
   d) Smoking and drinking? Okay or no-no?
10) Dealing with violations and conflicts
   a) Yell-out, freeze-out or time-out?
   b) Fighting dirty or clean?
   c) Analyse and understand the fight or talk about it?

     d) Who makes up? Is the first person to make up the loser or the winner?

     e) Abuse—zero tolerance or acceptable if occasional?

     f) Nagging and dominance? Acceptable, necessary or can be done without?

11) Children

     a) Yes, no, how many?

     b) When? When both of you are ready or when everybody around you wants you to have one?

     c) Parenting styles that are the most appropriate.

     d) Who takes the primary responsibility for the care of the child(ren)? How are child-caring tasks to be shared?

12) Values and belief systems

     a) At least three (more if possible) key values that your lives will be based on (values like honesty, concern for environment, family before everything else, etc.).

     b) Attitudes to religion and spiritual pursuits?

     c) How to deal with value conflicts or violations?

Please remember that the above is not a comprehensive list, only an indicative one. Please feel free to add on any more parameters that both of you see fit. But make sure you cover at least all the 12 major parameters listed above.

SOME GUIDELINES FOR TEMPLATE DEFINITION

As both partners talk about the way they have perceived their parents treating each other along the parameters listed above (and perhaps, more that they can come up with), they will realise that their own expectations of each other have been substantially governed by their respective parents' marriage templates. At this time they need to decide which of the elements, if any, of their parents' templates they would like to adopt in their final marriage template. But this process, unless done rationally, can cause more conflict than it needs to, as happened to Nikhil and Anita.

Anita came from a relatively sheltered, but liberal, background in that she was treated like a princess by her parents. Her parents, who had an amicable divorce when Anita was twelve, both loved her dearly, and tended to spoil her a bit. She was more used to receiving than giving and as a result, tended to be a little self-centred in her relationships. Since she had a couple of boyfriends when she was growing up, her self-centredness was a little tempered by the time she got married. As she was a very warm and compassionate person, Nikhil tended to ignore any tantrums that she threw. However, he came from a conservative background and his image of marriage was quite different. His parents had clearly defined roles—his father was the provider and his mother the homemaker. In all matters pertaining to the children, the father deferred to her wisdom, although by no means was he a distant father to Nikhil and his two brothers. Nikhil had grown up with very clear-cut expectations of the role he had to play when he got married. Needless to say, both their primary marriage templates were in conflict with each other. Anita believed that hers was a superior one, and expected Nikhil to adopt it in totality. He was resistant to this, because she was getting him to do so, not through rational discussion, but by becoming petulant, throwing tantrums and even getting his friends to persuade him to adopt her line of thinking. As a result, they couldn't define their optimal final marriage template for a long time.

Finally, they adopted the following guidelines, and had an easier time defining their final template.

a. If your primary marriage templates are very dissimilar, this does not mean you're incompatible; it just means you come from different places and have to work a little harder at defining your final template.

b. What worked for your parents may not necessarily work for both of you because they lived in different times and had lower expectations of each other.

c. Your husband is not your father, nor your wife your mother. So, expecting your partner to behave like your opposite-gender parent is irrational.

d. There are no rights or wrongs in defining your
    final template. If both of you feel it will work,
    you are on the right track.

e. Try and accommodate your partner's needs to
    the extent you can. If you find your partner's
    needs irrational, express it, but do so with
    compassion, not aggression.

f. Despite this, if your partner is very keen on
    incorporating an irrational element into the
    template, and as long as both of you are clear
    that the requirement comes from an irrational
    place, and the adjustment required to
    incorporate it into the template is not back-
    breaking, I would recommend you try and fit
    it in. Like irrational expectations, these
    requirements too may die down in course of
    time. Jyotsna was very keen that her fiancé
    Samir never trouble her with his business
    worries because she felt that her father's
    constant complaining about problems in his
    company had made her mother a nervous
    wreck. Samir thought this was irrational, since
    he believed husbands and wives should share
    everything with each other, as his parents had
    done. When they discussed the matter, both
    agreed that sharing was very important, but
    Jyotsna was still uncomfortable about sharing
    his work anxieties. Much to her relief, he
    decided to go along with her requirements.

Within a few months of their getting married, she became an active part of his business and shared not just his worries, but also the responsibility of running the company.

g. Your final template need not look anything like your respective primary templates. It can look completely different.

h. In choosing which elements of your respective primary templates you will absorb into your final template, resist the temptation of saying, 'For every one item from your primary template, one from mine, too'. It is quite conceivable that the parents of one of the partners had a more balanced marriage than those of the other. This does not mean that the latter's parents are being let down, ignored or marginalised in the development of the final template. Your final template should be about what is best for both of you, not about whose parents had a better marriage. Keep your egos out of this exercise.

i. Even if one or both partners come from a divorced background, their primary templates are still rich sources of information in developing the final template, and should not be discarded on the grounds of parental divorce. In fact, if the parents had an amicable divorce and are still good friends with each other, there is much that can be learned from their marriage.

j. If the two of you cannot agree on any particular element, don't sweat about it. Keep it on the pending list and try and review it as you get closer to each other in later years. For example, Nikhil's parents never displayed their affection for each other in public, or even private, as far as he could tell. Anita's parents had no bones about hugging each other even in their children's presence. Nikhil felt hugging and kissing were activities that were strictly to be confined to the bedroom, and could not bear the thought of even holding hands at a party. After much discussion, they agreed that they would go with his comfort level, even if it meant that Anita had to make a conscious effort to touch-him-not in public. Over the initial year of marriage, as each started relaxing in the other's company and the two got closer to each other, Anita found him holding on to her when they went out. Smart wife that she had by now become, she didn't make a hue and cry about this change. She just quietly enjoyed it.

k. After discussing their respective primary templates, both partners may eventually feel that they may want to create a completely fresh final template for themselves, which does not reflect their primary templates at all. If such is the case with you, by all means go ahead and do so.

Let me reiterate something. Defining the final template is not one smooth process that a couple performs over an evening sitting down with pen and paper. It happens over a period, when one is faced with situations where one has to make choices or take calls. However, if you keep the above parameters and principles at the back of your mind, you might find it easier to take those tough decisions instead of waffling over them or ignoring them altogether. Needless to say, keeping the final template in place is quite energy-intensive. You might find that every now and again, you slip into earlier modes of functioning, based on your primary template. If you catch yourself doing this, don't be surprised. It happens to all of us. Sometimes, your partner may remind you that you're slipping. Don't get mad. If there is truth to this, just accept it and move on. I know a couple who, after defining their final template, reduced it to a vision statement for their marriage, which they printed out, laminated and kept with them all the time. Whether you need to do this or not, I don't really don't know, but if it works for you, by all means go ahead.

Also, do remember that the final template is likely to get refined over the years. So because you've developed a final template in the first year of marriage, doesn't mean you are doomed to living with it for all time to come. What the final template does is to give you starting anchor-points, and permits both of you to create a marriage space that is sensitive and responsive to each other's needs. The template provides you a conducive environment for growth. As you grow as human beings, your increasing maturity will ensure that your template also matures with you.

One last reminder on template definition. Your final template will work only when you

- prioritise your marriage and allocate adequate time for it
- don't fear becoming dependent on your partner
- are not resistant to change by your partner, and
- keep in mind the four golden rules of clarifying expectations.

9

The 'I' Space

If you have gone through the process of defining the 'We' space or the marriage space, you might have already touched on some of the elements that would constitute your respective 'I' spaces or personal spaces. However, whatever you disagreed on in the marriage template definition process are not the only contents of the personal space. The 'I' space is not a wastebasket category, and would also require some conscious attention.

ARE PERSONAL SPACES REALLY NECESSARY?

A few young couples deep in the throes of love sometimes feel that personal spaces are not necessary. They feel the need to merge both their identities and function as two halves of one big whole. Neither feels complete without the other and each feels compelled to participate in even the smallest aspect of the other's life. Sooner rather than later, they end up smothering and stifling each other. I think Deepa's story (*in the preceding chapter*) may have persuaded you that personal spaces are necessary, even critical in a relationship. We must remember that two independent identities have come together to create a marital unit. And the integrity of the respective identities should never be compromised. Unfortunately, in our country, short shrift is given to the woman's identity once she gets married. There are even some communities where the woman is expected to change her first name once she gets married, signifying that she is discarding her pre-marital identity completely to metamorphose into a wife. Now, if the man did likewise, this would mean that both were forsaking their respective pre-marital identities to forge new ones, and lend some parity to the process. However, this is not the way to go either, for marriage is not about creating fresh identities, it is about working with what you have, and forging a new style of functioning, a new togetherness, as it were.

By the time we get married, our personalities have already formed and while we are still perfectly capable of changing our attitudes, beliefs and prejudices to create a new pattern of communication, our basic personality characteristics are unlikely to change.

As Anil discovered when he married Beena. She was and continues to be a finicky person, obsessively clean, meticulously tidy and very well organised in her affairs. Shortly after their wedding, she set about clearing up Anil's cupboard, his desk and all his affairs in right earnest. Initially he was pleased, but when he realised that all his papers were placed in colour-coded files, his clothes were arranged in combinations and even his condoms were organised by colour as well as expiry date, he got edgy. He thought she was overdoing it. Perhaps she was, but she couldn't prevent herself. If she didn't organise things this way, she experienced a great internal anxiety and discomfort and it would nag away at her mind until she did. In an attempt at 'curing' her, he tried to make her life as difficult as possible by leaving his wet towel on the bed, his freshly ironed clothes strewn all over the floor and his papers in a mess.

Initially this upset her terribly, but after a while, she patiently cleaned up after him, sometimes doing so till late at night. She could not go to sleep if something had not been put away in its right place. In all other ways, both of them got along excellently, even though her insistence that he have a bath and clean his teeth before they made love (she showered before and after sex) and her pointblank refusal to engage in oral sex did irritate him a bit. They recognised that their fights were over small and petty issues, but they still fought over the same things, principally her obsessiveness. Not able to deal with this, Anil took Beena to see a psychiatrist, who, after examining her, explained to him that Beena had some obsessive traits in her personality, that these were perfectly normal, and suggested that since she only expected his cooperation in cleanliness, he should take it in his stride and do his bit to keep their environment tidy. Beena continues to be obsessive and Anil, having learned to give her the space to be what she is, stopped trying to make her over to what he thought she should be, and now realises how much her traits have benefited both of them. They have never fought over this issue since.

So, what then is this personal space? Just like the marriage space, it is a mental thing. It refers to recognising the fact that each partner in a relationship is entitled to have their own package of attitudes, beliefs, likes and dislikes, prejudices and interests that are unique to the individual. Merely because two people are married does not mean that either or both partners will have to give up any of these to forge a completely new package that both are comfortable with. Further, there is an understanding that each one may change the elements that constitute their respective package from time to time; this is bound to happen as one grows. But this change happens at the instance of the individual and not the partner. In other words, by seeing the way you handle something, your spouse may find your approach more effective and may try to do it your way, but when you insist that yours in the only way, then you're definitely encroaching on your partner's space.

There is a popular belief that for a marriage to take off, couples should have the same interests. Hardly true! While it is always nice if they share some interests, they don't need to give up their past interests unless they tire of them. There are always new interests that can be developed together.

Actually, the concept of 'I' space was recognised even in our parents' time, even though it was not called 'personal space'. Sending the wife to her parents' place for the birth of the child served not only to relieve her of her household chores but also to give her some breathing space where she could return to a pre-marital type of lifestyle. There was also a well-established practice of the wife taking the children to her parents' home for the summer vacation, while the husband stayed behind and joined them just for a few days at the most. This too, served the same purpose.

HOW MUCH PERSONAL SPACE?

How big should the partners' respective personal spaces be in relation to the marriage space, is the next issue that needs to be explored. As has been said before, one needs to make sure that the two personal spaces in a marriage should neither come in each other's way, nor compromise the marriage space. Typically, in contemporary marriages, we find the following space distributions:

Type A: I we I—very large personal spaces and a very small marriage space

Type B: I we i—one very large personal space, one very small personal space and a very small marriage space

Type C: i we i—two very small personal spaces and a very small marriage space

Type D: i **WE** i—two very small personal spaces and a disproportionately large marriage space

Type E: I WE I—two clear and equal personal spaces with a substantial, though not disproportionately large marriage space (optimal).

When Shalini, a top manager in a multinational company, finally agreed to get married, she was 32. She felt her career path was safely established and she was financially stable. Her single-minded pursuit of her career had left her little time for relationships and she was beginning to feel a bit lonely every now and again. So she asked her parents to find somebody for her. They jumped at this and after much searching, finally found Rahul, aged 39, whose profile matched Shalini's perfectly. He was a finance professional who travelled a lot and was generally a loner by nature. He too was not averse to the idea of getting married. The two met, found that they were like two peas in a pod, and after receiving assurances from each other that neither would come in the way of the other's space, they got married.

Their lives continued as before. Hers was one big round of strategic meetings, review meetings, planning meetings, sales meetings and board meetings. He was flying to all the financial capitals of the world, busy raising funds, doing deals and making killings here and there. They met each other for about four days in a month, took time off from work, went to a different hill resort every time (they covered most of the country's well-known hill stations) and generally had a pleasant time in each other's company. The sex was happening, even if it was generally more a mechanical act, rather like brushing their teeth, than a passion-filled one.

Neither had too many complaints about this life, though. During the times they were apart, they pursued their own interests. He had a passion for opera, Formula One racing and antiquarian books, preferably first editions; she for Meissen porcelain, modern dance and collectible art. Neither particularly cared for the other's pursuits, but since they had a no-interference policy, neither said anything to the other. A year and a half into their marriage, Shalini felt that her biological clock was ticking, and on the advice of her gynaecologist, broached the subject of having a child on one of their monthly outings. He was aghast that she would ever want to consider such a thing. Having a child was not on his 'to do' list. And there was no way he was going to accede to her 'impossible' request. To play it safe, he stopped having sex with her.

This is a typical example of the type A space distribution (the I we I pattern) where both Shalini and Rahul had very substantial personal spaces but hardly anything in the marriage space. On the other hand, you find couples like Kalyani and Sabyasachi who were married when both were 25 years of age and moved in to live with Sabyasachi's joint family. Both were very busy trying to establish themselves in their respective careers: she was a psychologist and he a junior advocate. Whatever time they could spare from their busy working schedules went towards catering to the needs of their respective families (they were both only children of parents who ended up making a lot of demands on their time). As a result, neither had time for either their respective selves or each other, falling into the Type C (i we i) space distribution category.

I think you would have, in the course of your own lives, seen enough illustrations of Type B and Type D marriages, and hopefully of Type E marriages as well, for that is the space distribution format we need to aspire to. Many couples do successfully work out Type E patterns in the course of their married lives. Of course, we need to remember that the two 'I's may not often be absolutely identical to each other, but as long as they are close, things will work out fine and neither partner will feel short-changed.

In defining how large your personal space should be, you should first decide how much time you are in a position to commit as being exclusively yours. This has to be a joint decision since time is a premium commodity nowadays. It is quite true that different people have different time and space requirements. Some may need more, and some hardly any. So, the best way to go about it would be to first define your marriage space and the time you need to commit to that space, and then try and work out personal space requirements.

WHAT HAPPENS INSIDE YOUR PERSONAL SPACE

What you do with and in your personal space, is entirely your business. It is something you have rightfully earned by virtue of committing yourself to the relationship and by allowing your partner equal rights in the relationship. However, do bear in mind that whatever you do, you have to do within a common value framework. For instance, if all you want to do in your personal time is to surf porn on the Internet, and your partner finds this a particularly offensive thing to do, and this personal space activity of yours comes seriously in the way of experiencing quality marital space, then maybe it's time you reviewed it, don't you think?

The whole idea of personal space is that it stands for something that is exclusively yours. Some people feel compelled to fill their personal space with a large number of activities just because the space exists. And eventually, the personal space activities start expanding and filling up the marriage space as well. The very purpose of having personal space is that you have an opportunity to recharge yourself. Unfortunately, many of us tend to use our personal space and time to engage in activities that we cannot engage in when the spouse is present. When we do this, we crowd our personal space with activities that tire us rather than recharge us.

Since Kusum, a 30-something fabric designer, did not get along with his parents, Manoj, her husband, did whatever he could to keep his biological family and his nuclear family separate. Kusum and he reached an understanding that she had no problem with his doing things for his parents, provided she was not expected to participate. So, Manoj spent all his spare time looking after his parents' needs, like paying their utility bills, taking care of their health-related requirements, taking them out to visit their families and friends, and so on. All this, even though his younger brother was living with the parents and had enough surplus time to do all that Manoj was doing. However, Manoj felt the need to do all this to assuage the guilt he experienced because he was not in a position to support his parents financially. Even though he knew that they were comfortable, he felt it was his duty as the older son to take care of their financial needs. As a result, Manoj had no time for himself at all, and Kusum would always get upset with him when he was too tired to socialise with her over the weekend.

Do not underestimate the need for recharging your batteries. In today's life, what with long working hours, killing commutes, back-breaking financial commitments and hectic socialising, you will tend to burn out much sooner than did your parents. A one-week annual vacation doesn't really recharge you for the rest of the year. You need to engage in some preventive maintenance.

And the best thing you can do is to engage in some soul-nourishing activity. Many young people today tend to use their personal space in front of the television set or on the Internet. Frankly, if you ask me, this is a waste of your precious personal space. By all means watch TV or surf the Net, but let this not be the only activity that you pursue, for both are essentially mind-numbing activities than mind-expanding ones. Engage in activities that give you a sense of personal joy and accomplishment. Whether this involves yoga, meditation, reading, doing crossword puzzles or Sudoku, painting, making pots, writing poetry, doing theatre, volunteering your time at a suicide helpline, journaling and/or blogging your thoughts, or learning something new like a foreign language or the salsa, will depend entirely on personal tastes. All you need to remember in choosing your personal space activities are two things: one, the activity should give you joy and a sense of calm, and two, the activity should not become an obsession that progressively takes up more and more of your time and energy. If you enjoy Sudoku for instance, just enjoy it, don't obsess about becoming the next world Sudoku champion.

The biggest threat to the 'I' spaces in a marriage is something that is inherent in all human beings: the need to control our partners. Each partner feels the need to quickly establish who the boss in the marriage is, and as a result, several distracting control games get played out in contemporary marriages. Unless we try and understand why this happens and how we can stop trying to control our partners, our 'I' spaces are going to be difficult to define.

10

Who's the Boss? Control Games, Boundaries & Personal Space

It may, on the face of it, appear absurd that two people who have made a commitment to live with each other for the rest of their lives would attempt to control each other. But this is what all of us do, in our own ways. In fact, probably the first thing that many people attempt to do when they get married is either to make sure that their partners don't dominate them, or, as a pre-emptive measure, try and establish their dominance over the partner. 'Who's the boss?' often becomes a very emotive issue in the marriage because of the popular, though fallacious, belief that one partner should have the last say in any contentious issue in the marriage. Also, there is a popular cultural belief that men should be the dominant partner in a marriage, and even if the man is actually relatively mild during the courtship, he ends up becoming domineering soon after the knot is tied. Many young brides are mystified when their hitherto gentle, sensitive and romantic suitors suddenly turn into demanding, aggressive and insensitive husbands.

Mythili and Charan had a wonderful courtship. She had been very open with him about her difficult relationship with her father who was abusive, strict and extremely controlling of her and her sister. She had also told him of her two earlier relationships with men, which broke up when they acted macho with her. Charan was wonderfully sympathetic to Mythili and steadily broke down her defences. She slowly started to believe that she had found her ideal mate, a man who was willing to accept her as she was, and to let her be the way she was. In course of time they got married. Not even a month into the marriage, he started behaving strangely. Initially he insisted that she tell him her programme for the day, saying he felt more comfortable if he knew exactly where she was. Still in a bit of a romantic haze, she interpreted this as loving behaviour and went along. Soon he started getting miffed with her when she omitted telling him even minor details of what happened during the day. He wanted to know whom she spoke to and what she said to them.

Then, one day, he forbade her from having coffee with her colleagues after work, for this was unnecessarily delaying her return home. He went ballistic if she was not at home when he came back from work, for he liked her to give him something to eat and a massage so he could unwind. He controlled the family finances and decided the monthly budget. He also decided where they went out for dinner by shooting down all her suggestions and finally coming up with a venue that he probably wanted to suggest right at the outset. He insisted she switch her mobile phone off when she came back from work, just as he did. He made a big fuss if she went out with any of her friends without him. He hated it when she asked him to do anything for her in the presence of any of his family members or friends, and was openly rude to her when she did this. The coup de grâce came when he insisted that she let him manage her bank accounts and investments, and also tell him her e-mail account password, so there would be complete transparency between the two of them. As he pointed out to her, when she remonstrated with him, he was not asking her to do anything that he was not willing to do himself. Though this was true, she was not comfortable at all. His argument, that she would do all this for him if she really loved him, confused her, for she did love him, but was not ready to give up her privacy just to suit his needs.

Charan was very wily in the manner in which he tried to establish his dominance over his wife. He made sure that whatever he asked her to do, he was prepared to do himself. Not all men take that much trouble. Many simply expect their wives to 'obey' them and 'serve' them, and usually use the well-worn, but still serviceable, 'Indian culture' explanation to defend their behaviour. And amazingly, they receive support even from the other female members of the family when they do. In fact, men are often exhorted by their mothers and sisters to 'take charge' of the wife before she 'sits on your head'. Even if the man does not necessarily feel the need to dominate his wife, unable to withstand the pressure around him, he generally displays some form of machismo in his marital life. Of course, there are many men who don't really need the pressure to do so and are keen, themselves, on establishing that they are the bosses in their married lives.

Then there is the man who says, ' I *allow* my wife' to do a lot of things, without realising that it is not his role to 'allow' his wife anything. But equally, there are women who 'give their husbands permission to drink once a week'. Though generally it is men who tend to be the aggressors in our country, there are many women who can match them blow for blow. Such women quickly establish their position of supremacy in the relationship and crack the whip every now and again just to make sure the husband does not get any ideas.

Typically, the controller tries to cut off all the support systems of the partner to ensure that the latter has no one else to turn to in moments of distress. This is also what Charan tried to do when he attempted to cut Mythili off from her friends, thereby increasing her dependence on him. Many men insist that their wives have no further contact with their families, or attempt to restrict contact to the minimum, in order that back-up support systems are cut off. Here the belief is that this is the only way to ensure that the wife accepts him and his family as 'hers'. And it is usually seen as the role of the newly-married man to make this happen. This is largely because of the prevalent sub-cultural need for the man to be seen as the dominant partner in the marriage. As a result, even apparently mild-mannered men attempt, soon after the wedding, to stamp their authority on the wife.

Aside from this, there is another reason why both genders feel the need to dominate the relationship. Usually, when one gets married, one realises that one's life has changed forever. What hitherto constituted one's personal space, now has to be shared with another person. Even if the new element in our space is someone we love, there is a fear that the other may take our space over completely and do it up to suit their own requirements, paying scant attention to our needs. Also, when we get married, we experience a need for affirmation from the partner. This, therefore, puts us in a position of vulnerability. Normally, when human beings feel vulnerable, they either run away from the situation, or try and control it. Since it is usually difficult to run away after one is married (although, it must be said, many modern men and women do this with much success), one tends to try and establish control over the partner who is seen as the one causing the vulnerability. However, we don't really realise that the partner is trying to do pretty much the same thing to us.

One may ask why one allows oneself to be controlled by the partner? Does this reflect low self-esteem? Not always. Sometimes, one allows oneself to be controlled largely because it becomes the easy way out and one gets tired of resisting. Sometimes, an individual permits control because there is nowhere else to go or nothing else that can be done. And oftentimes, one allows oneself to be controlled because one has lower self-confidence than has the controller, a fact that the latter senses and exploits. This lower self-confidence is because we tend to value accomplishments and achievements more than core strengths.

Ashwin was a star. He was good looking and had an IIT-IIM background. On top of this, he was the youngest vice-president of a soft drinks multinational and an amateur scratch golfer. He considered himself an 'excellent catch' in the marriage market and expected Rina to be grateful that he chose her over several other contenders, even though she, an all-India rank-holding chartered accountant who had cleared both the intermediate as well as the final examination in the first attempt, worked for an international accounting firm and could not be considered any less accomplished than he was. However, his salary was higher, he was in the press more often and he got to travel much more than she ever would. Also, she tended to dress down and appeared frumpier than she needed to be. As a result, Ashwin felt that he was the more accomplished of the two and therefore deserved more consideration and respect, more so because the work he was doing was significantly more contributory to the economy than mere 'number-crunching'.

Despite being a spirited person, Rina agreed with his assessment of himself and of her, and within months, he called the shots at home. It was made explicitly clear that she would have to take primary responsibility for the home, including children whenever they decided to have some. She was also expected to ensure that her career did not come in the way of her homemaking responsibilities. He took all the decisions in their lives, because he was the one who understood revenue and finance; she was a 'mere accountant'. From where he stood, he had a great marriage. He did everything he wanted to—work, entertain, play golf, read—and his wife took care of everything else. From where she stood, she had no personal space and had to juggle multiple roles in her life with marginal support, if any, from her husband. Yet, she felt that she had to do what he wanted her to!

METHODS OF CONTROL

There are various ways in which people control each other. There is the kind of control we discussed earlier, where husbands expect their wives to 'obey and serve' them. Such husbands usually exercise *active control* on their partners. They generally tend to be up-front about their requirement that the partner plays, or is at least seen to play, a subordinate role in the marriage. Partners of such men can either be submissive to their lords and masters, can retaliate strongly (as in recent times many do), or they could exercise *passive control* over the men by apparently catering to their needs, but actually subtly manipulating the men to get their own way.

Passive control is something we, as a nation, are very good at. It involves non-cooperation, 'forgetting' to do what the partner expects, procrastination and manipulation, with absolutely no display of explicit aggression or control. Whether one tries to control one's partner actively or passively doesn't really matter. Control comes in the way of closeness between partners and reflects a lack of respect for the partner's identity and need for personal space. It goes without saying that controlling individuals ensure that their own need for personal space is properly taken care of.

There are three key methods that couples in our country commonly employ to control each other: *emotional blackmail, nagging* and *intellectual battering*.

Emotional blackmail is a very powerful method of passive control. Since in our country we tend to control more passively than actively, we, particularly our mothers, have refined the practice of this method to a fine art. For emotional blackmail to be successful, an element of martyrdom has to be established. This happens typically through the sustained display of sacrifice of one's personal needs in the interest of the partner.

Parvati, who had learned the art of emotional blackmail from her mother, used it ingeniously to get what she wanted. First, she established her martyrdom in the mind of her husband, Shankar, by serving him dutifully, uncomplainingly taking care of all his mother's irrational requirements, lovingly tending to his mentally retarded brother, and giving in to all his sexual needs without making a fuss. She established herself as a real trooper in his mind, since she did all these things at great cost to her frail health. When his mother died, she used her martyrdom to slowly but steadily emotionally blackmail him into leading the rest of their lives the way she wanted. Every time he resisted, she would develop a bout of physical illness and artfully contrive to remind him of everything she had done for his mother.

It is never easy to determine whether emotional blackmail is engaged in consciously and wilfully or unknowingly and unconsciously, for sometimes, attempts at emotional blackmail appear to be pretty brazen. But whether it is done consciously or not, it does constitute manipulative behaviour. Eventually, the 'victim' will start recognising the patterns, and react with an eruption of suppressed resentment that can permanently damage the marriage.

Nagging, on the other hand, is a more blatant and conscious method of active control over one's partner. There is a popular belief that nagging one's spouse to do the 'right things' is perfectly acceptable in the Indian marriage. Mothers teach their daughters that, in the face of 'irresponsible behaviour' on the part of the spouse, the wife, in the interest of the family, should badger the husband into submission. This she is expected to do, by relentlessly pointing him in the right direction and leading him away from the temptation of going down the 'wrong path', for instance alcoholism, 'womanising', and so on. Fathers teach their sons to 'control the wife' using any means available, including nagging. As a result, many newly married couples nag their partners to do what they believe are the 'right things'. However, the New Indian Marriage does not accept nagging as a legitimate communication tool, because it is perceived as a violation of one's personal space, for rarely is nagging confined to 'right things'. It becomes a pattern of communication and control, and once one achieves some success with this method, one invariably adopts it as a regular behavioural pattern.

Intellectual battering is a control method adopted

with increasing regularity by urban couples. Typically, one of the partners is more intellectually gifted, or at least better informed than the other. The more 'intellectual' partner wears down the less 'aware' one through interminable discussion, irrefutable (sometimes even perverse) logic and rational discourse. On the face of it, the 'battered' partner cannot really take umbrage at the other, for there are no apparent coercive tactics being employed. Everything seems very rational and logical, and discussion is always encouraged. However, if every trivial action or behaviour is to be subject to intense intellectual scrutiny using parameters that seem incomprehensible, many people just give in. This pattern of control is a subtle form of emotional abuse (*discussed in a later chapter*), for it erodes the confidence and self-belief of the partner over time.

Whatever is one's preferred vehicle of controlling one's partner, I can tell you that, at some point of time in the relationship, the controlled partner will either rebel against or drift away from the controlling partner. If you're reading this book, I assume that this is not the fate you want for your marriage. If this is the case, a resolution to respect your partner's personal space even if you're not completely comfortable doing so, is your best bet to ensure that your marriage lasts the distance. This way, genuine respect can enter the relationship and as you grow closer to each other, whatever niggles exist will be ironed out, thereby creating the possibility that your spouse can become a friend and a companion. When you're older, your parents are long gone and your children are busy establishing their own lives, believe me, it's only the companionship that you and your spouse have built up over the years that will still remain to see both of you through the rest of your lives. To ensure this companionship, it would be a good idea to consciously look at boundaries in your marriage.

BOUNDARIES AND PERSONAL SPACE

How private you want to keep your personal space is basically your call. Should your partner have access to your blog? Should you introduce your Spanish class buddies to your spouse? Should your spouse know your e-mail password or is this to be exclusive to you? Should you share with your partner the contents of a personal sms from an opposite-gender friend? How much of your 'self' are you comfortable 'exposing' to your spouse? How much ingress are you willing to permit your spouse to your personal space? How much privacy do you feel you need? Another way of looking at it is, how much you are willing to extend yourself for your spouse at this point of time in the relationship? This is what is meant by defining relationship boundaries.

Simply put, a relationship boundary tells us how much we are prepared to open our arms and accommodate a particular individual in our lives; how much we are prepared to extend ourselves for this individual. It is not a *lakshman rekha* that we use to tell our partner 'thus far and no further'. In fact, it has nothing to do with the partner at all. It is just a pointer to ourselves that, at this particular stage of life, this is how much we can comfortably (without breaking our backs), extend ourselves for this individual. All our relationships have boundaries, whether with our parents, friends, children or spouse. This is why we are usually willing to extend ourselves more for one parent than the other, more for a spouse than a friend, and so on. Usually, we are not conscious of how and when we erect these boundaries, and therefore, run the risk of taking them for granted. It's perfectly understandable that our childhood boundaries were unconsciously defined, but since marriage is a relationship we engage in when we're adults, it would be appropriate to be a little more conscious when we define our boundaries with our spouse.

In defining your relationship boundaries with your spouse, try and keep the following guidelines in mind.

1) *There are no right and wrong boundaries, only congruent and incongruent ones.* If both partners are comfortable with a boundary, it becomes congruent and poses no problem. Since Kusum was comfortable with Manoj not involving her in his relationship with his parents, and Manoj also went along with this, this can be considered

a congruent boundary. It is quite possible that to one of their friends, this may appear to be a wrong way of handling things. However, that still does not make Kusum's and Manoj's boundary wrong or inappropriate. If it works for them, no problem. If it doesn't, then they'll obviously have to talk through it. In other words, if something is working for you and both of you are genuinely comfortable with it, don't waste your time fiddling with it. For instance, if both of you know each other's e-mail passwords and download each other's mail whenever needed, but your friend is horrified that you've allowed your spouse so much ingress into your privacy, don't break your head over it. Don't second-guess yourself trying to figure whether you need to increase your privacy levels. Each of us has different privacy needs, and what doesn't appeal to your friend can work perfectly fine for you. There is no such thing as a formula for how private you must be.

2) *Boundaries can be tight or relaxed.* People who, for whatever reason, need more privacy than others, generally tend to draw their boundaries very close and very tightly around themselves. In other words, they are very private and very guarded. Some of us may be quite the opposite—generally blasé about how much the

partner knows—and are quite comfortable sharing a whole lot of personal details with the spouse. Most of us fall somewhere in between these two extremes. Our need for privacy depends on a combination of factors: childhood experiences, personal values, other relationship experiences, what our favourite glossy has told us, what we've read about how open to be in a marriage, and so on. So, if some of us need more privacy, that's not a big deal. It's only when the partner makes a fuss about this, that things start getting sticky.

Many newly-married couples expect their partners to shed their inhibitions overnight and become immediate confidants. Give it some time. As partners get more comfortable with each other, tight boundaries will progressively loosen and eventually become relaxed. It's only when laxity is demanded as a right by one of the spouses, that things get out of hand.

3) *Boundaries change with time.* Our boundaries are not carved in stone; they are always changing. So one need not worry that the boundaries that exist in the beginning of a marriage will remain for the rest of one's married life. This applies to relaxed as well as tight boundaries. At some stages of your life, you may experience the need for greater privacy and a hitherto elastic boundary may become slightly tighter.

But this need not be a problem if both partners respect this and give each other space and time to loosen the boundary again.

4) *Inclusive and exclusive boundaries.* When Kusum defined a boundary in her marriage vis-à-vis Manoj's family, she paid scant regard to Manoj's feelings (of guilt etc.) on the matter of dealing with his parents. She defined an exclusive boundary. She effectively excluded her partner's needs while defining how much she was willing to extend herself for him. Even though the boundary is congruent (Manoj was comfortable with it), it may have helped him deal with his emotions better if, in some way, Kusum had tried to understand this need and responded to it. An inclusive boundary, on the other hand, is one which takes into consideration the partner's feelings, thoughts or ideas on the matter. The approach then is not just *'it's your problem and you'd better deal with it'*; it becomes *'it may be your problem, but is there anything I can do to help?'* To make this particular boundary more inclusive, Manoj and Kusum, if they agreed that Manoj's guilt needed some help, could perhaps together work out a format to distribute the tasks and errands involved in the care of his parents between Manoj and his brother.

5) *Boundary violations.* Even if boundaries are consciously defined, we do tend to violate

them every now and again. You may remember the story of Beena and Anil (the lady with obsessive traits whose husband requested a psychiatric assessment). When Anil agreed to accommodate her obsessive needs by doing his best to keep his physical environment clean, tidy and organised even though he had no personal need for such orderliness in his life, he defined an inclusive boundary and made it congruent for both of them. However, every now and again, he would slip a bit and do something messy. This constitutes a boundary violation, even if an unintended one.

Sometimes, we violate boundaries intentionally, perhaps out of anger, maybe out of spite, or even out of sheer contrariness. When such boundary violations happen, a fight invariably ensues. If both partners have agreed that reading each other's text messages is unacceptable, and if one catches the partner doing precisely this on the sly, a boundary has been violated and there are going to be consequences. If, however, we work out a pattern of dealing with boundary violations, things don't have to necessarily go downhill. It would be useful to remember that not all boundary violations are intentional, but if a repeated pattern of boundary violation persists, then one needs to sit down and review the boundary.

As a general rule, a good way to enhance the quality of a marriage is to ensure that there are as few incongruent, tight or exclusive boundaries as is humanly possible without, of course, compromising one's sense of personal space. What I mean is, do your best to extend yourself for your partner, but don't sell your soul. Needless to add, the fewer the boundary violations, the happier the marriage.

11

Sex and Intimacy

No discussion on marriage can be considered complete without addressing the twin phenomena of sex and intimacy. We tend to use both these terms interchangeably, but the two are quite distinct from each other although each has a strong bearing on the other. Sex, in its most primal form, is a biological phenomenon, a drive that exists in all human beings. It is usually considered a procreational drive, since its most manifest outcome is conception and therefore, propagation of the species. Sex is governed by sex hormones and sexual attraction by pheromones (chemical substances mixed in a person's odour that either attract or repel you). Sex is considered analogous to hunger and thirst as a basic human need, although in human beings, sex is a need that is not essential for survival of the individual, only of the species.

If it is indeed, a purely procreational activity, as it is considered to be by several religious denominations, it should not, strictly speaking, cause the kind of problems that it does. Men and women would have sex whenever their hormones dictated and life would go on. A corollary to this would be that, for as long as everybody was guaranteed as much sex as they wanted (as much procreational opportunities as they wanted), life would be harmonious and perfect. However, as we all know, this is not the way things work. We spend extraordinary amounts of time thinking about sex. Even when we have a regular sexual partner, we fantasise about having sex with somebody else. We can kill for sex. We are willing to pay astronomical amounts of money for sex. It is therefore reasonable to assume that sex is not merely a procreational activity.

Perhaps, because it is arguably the most pleasurable experience known to mankind, it should also be considered a recreational one. When an activity becomes recreational, it is no longer a matter of only hormones. When we eat, we gratify not merely our basic need of hunger, but cater to our higher epicurean taste. Likewise, when it comes to the basic need of sex, other elements enter the picture: ideas of beauty, sexiness, and an indefinable feeling of being comfortable enough with an individual to expose one's nakedness. All of these reside in your mind and your emotional state, and together engender the experience of *sexual intimacy*. This is different from emotional intimacy (*which we'll explore a little later in the chapter*), but it is sexual intimacy that elevates the sexual experience from a purely procreational act to a recreational one. Unfortunately, this elevation also brings with it a few problems and issues that result in the overall sexual experience being fraught with anxieties and misapprehensions based on misconceptions. As a result, many couples in our country experience the *Suhaag Raat Syndrome*, and many marriages in our country remain unconsummated for inordinately long periods.

THE SUHAAG RAAT SYNDROME

If your answer to the question, 'What do most Indian couples do on their suhaag raat?' is 'Sleep', you are absolutely correct. For this is what invariably happens. Few Indian marriages get consummated on the wedding night itself, and the stories that you hear from your friends and relatives about how many times they did 'it' on the wedding night are more than likely, exaggerated, and often plain fantasy. The odds are loaded against wedding night consummation. Indian weddings are big, fat, elaborate and exhausting affairs. Marriages are invariably solemnised at unearthly hours. The bride and the bridegroom are expected to have a rollicking time at the pre-wedding parties, the *sangeet*, the *mehndi*, the stag party, the hen

party and all sorts of other events that, by the time
the wedding day rolls along, they have over-indulged
themselves to the point of sickness. Also, they are
ready to drop. They probably need a holiday to recover
from the wedding. Little wonder then, that during the
wedding night and the ensuing honeymoon (if one
takes place at all), sex is not on top of the couple's to-
do list. Also, extraordinary as this may sound, it is not
uncommon to see parents and other family members
accompanying the newlyweds on the honeymoon.
Needless to say, sex and sexual intimacy have to
remain squarely on the back-burner.

However, this is not the only reason marriages are
unlikely to be consummated on the wedding night. In
arranged marriages, anxiety, nervousness and
apprehensions are the principal reasons why couples
tend to avoid engaging in sexual activity. Also,
considering the couple has hardly had any interaction
with each other, they are generally shy of each other.
In such a situation, it is hardly reasonable to expect
two relative strangers to throw themselves at each
other in a passionate clinch. In general, women, more
than men, require time to get to know their partners,
before they can engage in sexual intimacy.

In love marriages, the partners have invariably
engaged in some form or other of sexual activity. In
the metros and larger cities, couples are more likely to
have gone all the way and had penetrative sex with
each other, unless they come from a conservative

background, in which case, 'making out' and mutual masturbation seems to be more the norm. However, given the fact that, even in metros, single people tend to live with their parents, the lack of availability of a suitable sexual venue tends to ensure that pre-marital sexual activity is carried out furtively and clandestinely. As a result, not surprisingly, the suhaag raat syndrome may tend to make its appearance even in love marriages, with one important difference. In love marriages, since some form or other of sexual intimacy is established, couples find it easier to deal with the syndrome and establish a mutually satisfying sexual rhythm.

WHY IS IT SOMETIMES SO DIFFICULT TO CONSUMMATE THE MARRIAGE?

An inadequate appreciation of the confusion, misapprehensions and anxieties surrounding the whole issue of sex and sexuality has resulted in an increase in the incidence of unconsummated marriages in recent times. I have seen marriages that have gone on for as long as ten years without being consummated. Sadly, many couples go through years of marriage depriving themselves of the joy that good sex and intimacy can bring. Surprisingly, not all such couples look for a medical or psychological solution to this problem.

Usually, the first few months of a newlywed's life are dominated by sexual issues that manifest in a variety of ways. While a comprehensive discussion of sexual issues and problems is beyond the scope of this book, as is a discussion of satisfactory sexual practices, it would be prudent at least to have an overview of some of the more common misadventures that afflict newly married couples, in order that we may empower ourselves not to go down the same path.

Inadequate knowledge of sex

Padmini was an attractive young cub reporter with a local newspaper who entered into an arranged marriage with Vinay, a software engineer. He had a small-town background, but considered himself urbanised for he had lived in a metro for several years and had been sent by his company for two stints to the United States. Having had a fairly conservative upbringing in a traditional joint family, Padmini's knowledge of sex was limited to what she had acquired from Indian cinema, which, as we all know, tantalises more than it reveals. Two days before the wedding, an older cousin, who had been assigned the responsibility of sexually educating Padmini, attempted to give her a hasty sketch of what to expect, which ended up disturbing her and leaving her with more questions than answers. Her cousin advised her not to worry and to leave it to Vinay, who, it was assumed, would provide her with all the answers. Vinay's sexual knowledge had been obtained almost entirely from pornographic websites on the Internet. Despite being well-travelled, he had never had any personal sexual experience. But because he masturbated prolifically and had seen videos of couples in all the sexual positions known to man, he was pretty confident of his sexual prowess. Accordingly, on the suhaag raat (wedding night), he tried to do to Padmini what he had seen innumerable macho men do to the submissive women in porn videos. Foreplay was, needless to say, conspicuously absent. Since he had never been close enough to a woman to kiss her, and since porn stars do not really make a big deal about kissing, he tried to get on with the act straight away, thereby traumatising his young bride, physically and emotionally. The marriage was consummated in that penetration did take place, but since he had been so rough, she suffered from bruising and minor lacerations in her genital area and he tore the fraenulum of his penis, ensuring that neither wanted to have anything sexual to do with each other for a long time. Fortunately, the doctors both of them had to visit put them onto a sex therapist, who taught them some sexual basics, thereby salvaging what could have been a very unpleasant outcome.

It is quite astonishing that, despite living in a land where even the scriptures elaborate on the physical union of man and woman, we have such a poor knowledge of sex and such a puritanical approach to acquiring it. When sexual knowledge is obtained purely from dubious sources such as equally ill-informed peers, the Internet and pornography, it goes without saying that such knowledge is going to be distorted, unrealistic and confusing, among other things. Also, such misinformation tends to reduce sex to a less-than-wholesome act, rather than a pleasurable experience, and can end up putting people off sex, women more than men. Therefore, it would be best that both partners talk about their sexual knowledge or lack thereof, with as little embarrassment as possible, always remembering that, since we live in a sexually prudish society, most of us have inadequate information about sex. It may be appropriate to consult self-help books or talk to a sex educator or sex therapist to help you acquire the relevant knowledge.

Performance anxiety, erectile dysfunction and premature ejaculation

One of the most primal anxieties that give men nightmares is the fear of impotence. During different stages of their lives, men generally tend to experience different degrees of sexual arousal and interest. One of the reasons that most men want to have sex as soon as possible after the wedding, is to prove their virility and sexual capability. However, what we need to realise is that sexual arousal, although a physiological mechanism, is governed very strongly by our emotions. It's because of this that when one is worried, anxious, depressed or fearful, sexual arousal is extremely difficult. As we have already discussed, the whole wedding process is a fairly stressful occasion for both the man and the woman. As a result, it is not at all unusual for a man to find it difficult to get or maintain an erection in the early stages of marriage.

After the stress of the wedding celebrations, men often experience *performance anxiety*, because they feel they have to prove themselves to the woman as being worthy of marriage. At the very beginning, there exists a fear of failure in the minds of most men, which is also compounded by the ubiquitous *penis size problem*. Since many men resort to pornography, they are constantly overawed by the unnaturally endowed men on the screen. This starts making them feel inadequate about the size of their own penis. Also, their friends boast of having extremely large sex organs (exaggerated, more likely than not). Let me tell you something, gentlemen. Two inches of erect penis is more than adequate, for it is only the first couple of inches of a woman's vagina that are rich in nerve endings. And it is never how much you have, but how effectively you use it, that will determine the quality of your partner's satisfaction.

The first few times they tried to have sex, it appeared to Romila that nothing really happened. She had married Ranjan after a courtship of two-and-a-half years, during which period, she had never allowed him to touch her sexually. Occasionally, she had cuddled a bit with him, but nothing more than that. He had always seemed to be in a perpetual state of sexual arousal then, and she had looked forward to a happy sex life. But nothing seemed to be happening! Every time he approached her, she willingly reciprocated. But after caressing her a bit, he abruptly turned away and went to sleep. She started feeling that she was in some way repulsive to him. It was only when she discovered that he was surreptitiously washing his underclothes after each occasion that they'd come close, that she started probing and realised that Ranjan was ejaculating prematurely, even before he could attempt penetration.

Premature ejaculation in the early part of the sexual relationship is absolutely normal. This too is related to sexual performance anxiety as well as sexual inexperience. The heightened anticipation of sexual pleasure can put the individual in such a state of hyper-excitability that the climax turns out to be an anti-climax. And each time this happens, the man tends to feel miserable and inadequate, which in turn adds to his performance anxiety ('How will I be the next time?'), and a cycle establishes itself. Usually, as one has sex more and more often, the ejaculatory interval starts getting longer and the man can hold himself back for longer periods, thereby increasing his partner's pleasure as well. But until this happens, do provide for some amount of premature ejaculation and try satisfying your partner in other ways, either orally or by masturbation. However, if your premature ejaculation continues for more than a few months, I would recommend you visit a sex therapist or marriage counsellor, for there exist some very simple techniques that can set right the problem immediately.

Painful intercourse for women (dyspareunia)

The rough equivalent of erectile dysfunction in women is dryness of the vagina, which results in severe pain during penetrative sex. The dryness is on account of the fact that normal vaginal lubrication does not take place. Typically, inadequate lubrication is caused by anxiety and fear, as well as inadequate sexual stimulation (women need more stimulation than men to engage in sex). This is easily corrected by the application of some freely available vaginal lubricant jellies. Sometimes, the vaginal muscles can go into spasm and keep the orifice tightly shut, thereby preventing penetrative sex. This condition, called *vaginismus*, can have a variety of causes, but is often related to the psychological discomfort that some women have towards sex or to their partners. As said earlier, in an arranged marriage, it is more difficult for women to engage in such an intimate act with a relative stranger, and until she experiences emotional comfort with her new husband, vaginismus and dyspareunia are quite possible, Other causes of dyspareunia like pelvic infections, tough hymen, vaginal size etc., would require gynaecological evaluation. In other words, if dyspareunia and vaginismus persist even after a few months, then consult your gynaecologist. But more often than not, with some patience and some easing up of the discomfort between partners, these problems gradually disappear.

Prior sexual experiences

Sometimes, as Ganesh and Arpita found, prior sexual experience can actually cause problems in one's current sex life. She'd told Ganesh, shortly after they met, that she had been in a few relationships, none of which had really worked out. However, these were well and truly in her past, and ever since she met Ganesh, she was completely committed to him. She was a very attractive girl and Ganesh, who'd never been in a relationship with a woman before he met her, fell easily and intensely in love with her. He appeared not to care about her past, but actually he did. Not that he was judgemental of her in a moral sense, but he was terrified that, because she had benchmarks, she would find him lacking. So, for a long time, he avoided sexual contact with Arpita until, one day, she confronted him and, as women are very good at doing, got the truth out of him. Fortunately, they were able to talk it through and eventually engage in a normal sex life, but for a while it was really touch and go.

This then brings us to the question, if one has had prior sexual experiences, does one talk about them to one's partner? If you ask me, what happened in one's past is not something that really needs to cause trouble in one's present, but the problem is one never really knows how things will turn out, as Arjun discovered to his consternation. When he fell in love with Vandana, he realised that she was a bit of a romantic and full of ideas like 'there was only one man for every woman' and 'one could love only one person in one's life'. When she asked him if he'd ever loved or had a relationship with anyone else, he denied it. They had a charmed courtship that involved only making out, as she wanted to wait till after they were married, which he found endearing. As things turned out, on the day of the wedding, he realised that Maya, Vandana's cousin from the US, was someone he had had, when he was studying in the US, a torrid and passionate relationship with. Unfortunately, Vandana too realised that something was amiss, by the studied and elaborate manner in which the two of them avoided each other and the discomfort reflected in their body language when they found themselves together. Needless to say, she ferreted out the whole story from both of them independently. It was too late to do anything, since the marriage had already been solemnised, but she was devastated and just could not relate to him sexually even though she wanted to. It took them a long time to get over the fact that he'd had past sexual experiences that he had hidden from her. In reality, he had not really committed a crime or anything, but from her point of view, he had. So, do you tell your spouse about your past, or not? I leave it to you, but the general rule of thumb should be that only those details from the past that could impact on the present and the future need to be shared. The rest may be neither relevant nor important. However, even if you do feel compelled to make a 'clean breast', at least spare your partner the gory details.

Child sexual abuse

It is now well documented that the incidence of sexual abuse of children, especially girl children, is very high in our country (between one-third and one half of young girls have been exposed to at least one unsavoury sexual advance if not actual sexual exploitation). Although sex with minors amounts to rape in our statutes, rarely do such instances get reported, for more often than not, the abuser is an older relative. Often, as a means of dealing with the abuse, women tend to repress the event into their sub-conscious minds, but the experience does change the way they look at sex and sexuality. Usually two kinds of reactions to sex are seen by people who have been sexually abused. Some women end up becoming sexually promiscuous for they believe that sex is the only way they can give and receive love. But many women end up becoming repulsed by the sexual act, or at the very least, averse to it, for reasons that they are not immediately aware of. Women who have been sexually abused as children do need to spend some time in psychotherapy to deal with such a problem. Having worked with adult survivors of child sexual abuse, I can readily tell you that a supportive spouse is absolutely critical to the process of recovery. So, if you or your partner feels repulsed by or active aversion to the thought of having sex, despite both of you having established mutual comfort with each other, you might consider meeting a psychotherapist to explore the possibility of child sexual abuse.

ENHANCING SEXUAL TOGETHERNESS

I wouldn't really like to tell you how to conduct your sex lives, because the joy of sex comes from spontaneous explorations and serendipitous discoveries. However, I would like to tell you how you can level the playing field, thereby giving yourselves a chance to experience genuine sexual togetherness and sexual intimacy. When it comes to your sex life, these guidelines may help.

1) Educate yourself as much about sex before you get married, and use legitimate sources of information in doing so. Remember, porn may titillate, but will never educate. Don't get awed

by porn stars, who are very experienced at what they do, even if they make some very complicated positions look easy. Also, they become porn stars because they're very well endowed and do not represent the average body by any means. Additionally, they do use a lot of sexual aids that you're unaware of, which explains why they can go on for as long as they do. If you enjoy watching porn, that's your business, but let it not be your sex manual.

2) Try and approach your sex life with the intention of 'making love' to your partner rather than just 'having sex'. This subtle shift in emphasis ensures that you are as conscious of your partner's needs as your own. This makes for a more mutually satisfying process. If you are a man, this will help you remember that for women, sex is not a purely biological act, even if this is the case for you. A woman needs to feel emotionally connected to a man before she can even consider disrobing in his presence. So even if you've got a really hot body, don't expect your woman to necessarily be all over you; she will respond only when she feels emotionally connected with you and feels that you are emotionally tuning in to her. If you're a woman, remember that nowadays, even men need emotional comfort before jumping into bed. So if your partner is not

ready for you from day one, doesn't mean there's anything lacking in your sex appeal, it just means he, too, wants to make love, not have sex.

3) Talk sex. It's very important that partners talk about their attitudes, anxieties and concerns about sex. And when you talk, do not be judgemental about your partner, for nothing is more difficult to deal with and recover from than *sexual umbrage*. I'm not, of course, suggesting that you spend hours having intense, intellectual discussions about love-making. Just sharing your thoughts, feelings and expectations every now and again would do fine.

4) When you start love-making, concentrate on foreplay. Nothing is more important than learning the contours of each other's bodies, the nuances of each other's smell and a general feeling of relaxation in each other's presence. As said earlier, women generally need foreplay to get sexually aroused; they are not 'always on' like men tend to be. There are no fixed rules for foreplay. Do whatever you feel like doing and what your partner's comfortable with.

5) If penetration doesn't happen immediately, don't fret over it. Just give it some time. In the mean time, mutual masturbation will serve to

increase the bond. If you don't like what your partner is doing, try guiding appropriately. Remember, your partner will not know what you like, unless you articulate it.

6) If the man's erection doesn't happen, or if it cannot be sustained, don't panic. This happens to all couples. It's not because of his inadequacy or her lack of sex appeal. Just go back to foreplay until both of you are mentally relaxed and sexually aroused to try again. If nothing further happens that day, let it go. Try another time, when both of you are more relaxed.

7) When you're caressing or being caressed, tune out your thoughts. Instead, tune in to your body's sensations and start enjoying them.

8) If premature ejaculation occurs, it's no big deal. Just try and manually stimulate your partner. Remember that the more often you do it, the better you'll get at it.

9) When you complete love-making (whether penetrative or not), don't immediately rush to shower or turn over and go to sleep. *Afterplay* is as important as foreplay. This is the time when both of you are relaxed in each other's company, so you can snuggle, cuddle, horse around with each other, chat, or do whatever comes naturally to you. Afterplay also increases the bonding between partners.

10) Don't respond to what you read in magazines

and on the Internet regarding frequency, duration etc. of love-making. You're not practising for the Olympics, you're merely enjoying a natural act. What works for both of you is the right frequency, duration etc. What is most important is that both of you get into a sexual rhythm that both of you are comfortable with. Do remember that sex drives are variable, and one partner might want to make love more often than the other. My suggestion is to do your best to accommodate your partner's needs, but only if you comfortably can.

11) What you do in the privacy of your bedroom is your business, whether it's oral sex, or any other variation you might think of. One caveat though: both of you must be absolutely comfortable with what you're doing. No sexual act is a perversion between two consenting adults. However, if one partner is uncomfortable, pursuing the act would be completely unacceptable.

12) If you're not able to establish mutual sexual comfort with each other within six months of getting married, you would be well advised to see a good sex therapist or a marriage counsellor, who could help you resolve the bottleneck you find your sex life in. However, never exacerbate the matter by discussing it

with family and friends. This is a sure-fire recipe for disaster, for the resulting anger, humiliation and breach of trust would be very difficult to recover from. Remember, family members and friends are biased and emotional. Also, their knowledge of sex and sexuality may be limited at best, and distorted at worst. What you need is a professional who can understand the dynamics of the problem and help you resolve your issues. However, don't wait for too long before you seek help. The longer a problem pattern entrenches itself, the more difficult it is to change it. The most important thing is to accept that a problem exists, and that accepting this reality in no way diminishes the individual. In fact, when one accepts that there is a problem, one has taken the first and most important step to solving it.

If you take cognisance of the above guidelines and approach each other in a spirit of jointly exploring areas that were hitherto unknown to you, you will experience not only good sex, but also a mutually satisfying sexual intimacy that will go a long way in strengthening your bond with each other, as well as enhancing that other all-important element of marriage: emotional intimacy.

EMOTIONAL INTIMACY

The term 'intimacy' has not been a particularly significant part of the Great Indian Middle Class's lexicon until fairly recent times. Even today, when one uses the word, one usually refers to sex. This is quite a pity really, because while sex is indubitably an intimate act, intimacy goes far beyond the sex act. Unfortunately, given today's lifestyles, it does often come to pass that the only intimacy many urban couples share is the sexual encounter, which ends up being the chief agent of bonding between marital partners. As a result, couples tend to neglect 'emotional intimacy', an extremely important aspect of marriage that really makes the difference between whether partners tolerate each other's shortcomings or react angrily to them.

Intimacy is not 'romantic love' either. Although romance too is an expression of intimacy, the latter is much more than romance. Many couples fear that the fading away of romance from their relationships means the loss of intimacy. Not really true. As the relationship wears on, romance, as we define it, does tend to flag a bit. This is not because partners tire of each other, but because of the way we define romance. Flowers, cards and gifts have come to represent romance and have indeed become romantic rituals that most of us engage in. As a relationship wears on, these rituals, which are akin to 'mating rituals', will inevitably fade away. However, if the couple manages to get the relationship right, romantic love does get replaced by something more abiding, more fulfilling and more tranquil—emotional intimacy.

Intimacy is basically a feeling of closeness. As I see it, intimacy is more a feeling than a measurable act. It is the feeling of closeness between two people that makes even a mundane everyday kind of shared chore a relaxing, if not sublime experience. If you can do the dishes in companionable silence, without wishing you could break them over your partner's head, this is an intimate encounter. If you are able to tune into your partner's anxieties regarding a forthcoming presentation at work, this too is intimacy. In other words, it's not *what* the couple does but the *comfort* with which they do it that determines whether or not intimacy exists in the relationship.

Intimacy is about sharing emotions. Having said that intimacy is basically a feeling, it would naturally follow that both partners have to be in touch with their emotions if they are going to experience intimacy in the relationship. You can hardly be expected to feel intimately close to a partner who believes that emotions and demonstrativeness are a sign of weakness. The starting point of the experience of intimacy in a relationship is a belief that emotions must be experienced in depth and intensity, for it is in the sharing of these emotions that closeness and intimacy are actually experienced. The key issue here is not just the experience of the emotion, but its active sharing. There are many of the *strong silent type* of people who experience emotions with great intensity and richness, but have not learned how to express them. As a result, their experience of intimacy in close relationships becomes considerably constrained.

Intimacy is about signalling emotional needs. Often, when we experience some deep emotion, we expect our partners to magically understand what we are feeling, and respond appropriately. (*'If you really loved me, you would know how I feel'*). This is a bit harsh, really, for unless we *signal* our emotional needs in a manner that our partner can understand, it would be unfair to expect the right response. For instance, when one feels the need to be made a bit of a fuss of, one needs to signal this in a way that the partner can recognise. There's no point saying, *'I was so upset that I didn't eat the whole day, and you couldn't even be bothered'*, when there is no way of your partner's knowing that you haven't eaten. There are no right or wrong signals. There are only recognisable and unrecognisable signals. Each couple has its own private signalling codes and these can be refined through experience and discussion.

Intimacy is about tuning in to your partner's signals. There is no point developing an elaborate system of signals if both partners don't learn to tune into each other. Tuning into each other requires a conscious awareness of each other every time you're together.

By this I don't mean you follow each other around every evening, but just as a mother is finely tuned in to her baby's cry whichever room she is in, so too can you be tuned into each other's movements, activities and auras without actually imposing on each other. It takes a bit of practice, but it can be done.

Intimacy is about talking and listening to each other. Many couples end up talking *at* each other, not *to* each other. And they may 'hear' each other, although they hardly 'listen'. Their conversations tend to get ritualistic. This is why intimacy breaks down. If you think of your husband as a boring conversationalist, or he wonders when you're going to stop talking so he can get back to cricket on TV, these are not good ingredients for an intimate evening.

Intimacy needs time. Couples have to carve out enough time from their busy lives for intimacy. Hurried kisses and preoccupied hugs do not make for intimacy. One needs at least one 'intimacy evening' every week, when sans kids, sans friends, sans everything else, a couple can tune into each other, talk to each other, listen to each other, luxuriate in each other and enjoy each other. And the wonderful thing with an intimacy evening is that it does not need to be an expensive affair. You can eat peanuts at the beach, go for a long walk together, listen to each other's i-pods, and so on.

Keeping in touch through the day. In the age of mobile telephony, keeping in touch with each other through the day, even if the calls are brief, helps tremendously. This way, when you meet each other in the evening after a hard and tiring day's work, you don't feel like you have to start tuning in to each other from scratch. You are already in tune with each other, at least partially.

ENHANCING EMOTIONAL TOGETHERNESS

Emotional togetherness or intimacy does not come about automatically in a relationship; an emotional ambience geared to ushering in intimacy has to be consciously created. So the next time you feel that intimacy is taking a bit of a beating in your relationship, don't rush to the nearest book store to procure a copy of the illustrated *Kama Sutra*, just see if the guidelines below help you enhance the emotional intimacy in your marriage.

1. Remember to share your feelings and emotions with the one you love. Since intimacy is a feeling of emotional closeness, the more you learn to express your emotions, the more intimacy will you experience in your relationship. This is what Aruna realised when she married Raghav. Not given to expressing her emotions to anybody even though she was an emotionally intense person, she soon realised that every time she *did* show her love, Raghav would reciprocate with almost twice the warmth.

2.   Each of us, by virtue of childhood conditioning, has a different way of expressing or receiving positive emotions. It took a long time for Aruna to discover why Raghav was always complaining about her lack of interest in cooking. She'd told him right in the beginning that she was an indifferent cook and while she would supervise the housekeeping, she would hire the services of a professional in the kitchen. He seemed to go along with this when she'd first proposed it. But now, when both of them were exhausted at the end of the day, he would keep complaining about the quality of the food. Unfortunately, they had been extremely unlucky with the string of cooks they'd employed in the last few months. The only time Raghav seemed really happy with his food was on Sunday, when they went for lunch to his mother's house. It was only after much fighting and talking did Aruna finally realise that, all his pre-marital life, Raghav was used to love being shown to him through the vehicle of food, which was the only way his mother, like most Indian mothers, knew how to express her love (thereby, perhaps, explaining the Indian male's propensity to being overweight even at a young age). So, when Aruna was not cooking for him, some sub-conscious part of him interpreted this as her lack of love for him.

3. If you don't already know it, now is a good time to learn how to physically demonstrate your love and affection to your partner. In adult life, we need to develop different ways of receiving and expressing love. Perhaps the most effective method of expressing love is in non-sexual physical expressions such as holding, hugging, kissing, cuddling, and so on. Usually, when I ask couples whether they do any of these, the more urban ones tend to treat them as the most normal things to do, but a fairly large number of conservatives sanctimoniously inform me that only Westerners do such things, and that they see this as against Indian culture. Frankly, this is an argument I simply refuse to accept. How on earth can it be anti-Indian for a man and a woman who love each other, or are even growing to love each other, to show each other that they do, in the privacy of their homes or rooms? Intimacy needs to activate all one's sensory organs: sight, hearing, speech, smell and touch. Non-sexual physical demonstrations of affection are absolutely essential to couple-bonding and if you choose not to engage in them, you do so at your own peril!

4. You don't have to share emotions that you don't feel merely because you think your partner expects you to say nice things. If you

do this, your partner will see it as a sop and you will lose credibility. But every time you feel something positive, share it.

5. All of us are perfectly capable of expressing emotions. Remember how easy you find it is to blow up at your spouse when you're angry! Anger is also an emotion. If you have the wherewithal to express anger, so too can you express love. So, next time your partner comes up with the excuse of not being able to express emotions, you might want to look at the range of emotions that both of you express and explode this myth once and for all.

6. Expressing love is not a sign of weakness or mushiness. The more mature you are, the more you express your love for your partner.

7. When asked to express their love more often than they're accustomed to doing, some partners say, 'I married you, didn't I? Why should I keep on telling you I love you over and over again?' A hollow argument, really. Not saying, 'I love you' does not mean you love your spouse any less, but saying it means you are tuning into your partner's emotional needs and that you care enough to do so.

8. All human beings need periodic affirmation of affection, and the best way you can affirm that to your partner in marriage is showing you care enough to make the effort, in other words by being nurturing of your relationship.

9. Share the events of your day every day with your partner. This way, each of you knows what's happening in the other's life and you feel more connected to each other.

10. Stay connected with each other during the day or when you travel. Call each other at least a couple of times a day so you can touch base with each other even in a crowded day.

11. Don't expect your partner to assume your love. Show it.

12. When you're feeling down and troubled, is probably the best time to share your feelings, not with the intention of getting solutions, but just to feel your partner's love for you.

Sometimes, one partner is quite comfortable with the expression of emotional intimacy, while the other is distinctly uncomfortable, as Shehnaz found out when she married Xerxes. She had no real problem with him. He was a good provider and perfectly supportive when she told him she would prefer to be a homemaker than go to work. He had his own factory where he made chemicals, and worked hard, but always made sure he was home at a decent hour. He spent his weekends with her, took her to all their community get-togethers, bought her everything she wanted and was obviously perfectly comfortable with her. Sexually, too, he was attentive to her needs, even if he was not wildly passionate. He loved children and spent a lot of time playing with all the neighbours' children, who thoroughly enjoyed his company. However, he just couldn't verbally or physically express his love for Shehnaz. He attributed his lack of emotionality to growing up in an emotionally restricted family environment. What did Shehnaz do? I think she handled the situation brilliantly.

She didn't give up on him and never stopped trying to get Xerxes to become more expressive. She realised that in his case, lack of emotional expressiveness was not a character trait; it was only a result of his childhood conditioning. Or else, how could he express emotions so well to children?

She never pressured or 'nagged' him to communicate. She just went ahead sharing her own feelings with him and, by asking a few pointed questions, got at least a gist of what was on his mind.

Every now and again, she planned 'intimacy evenings'—not romantic getaways, but just a couple of quiet evenings during which each luxuriated in the other's company, even if not much was said to each other. The mere act of being together facilitated the slow onset of intimacy.

She stayed in touch with Xerxes at least a couple of times during the course of the day. However, he couldn't always take her calls in the factory and would therefore have to return her calls. Over a period of time, they mutually agreed that he would make the calls. He diligently did. She learned to recognise his signals for wanting privacy and respected them. He appreciated this and spent progressively less time in his private space.

Non-sexual physical contact was always important to Shehnaz. A hug, a kiss, a held hand. Initially, he thought of these more as chores, but she didn't mind. She figured that, sooner than later, these would become an indelible part of his repertoire as well. They did.

Most importantly, *Shehnaz never gave up on Xerxes.* Some people are harder to draw out than others, but nobody is impossible to draw out. And Xerxes is living testimony to this.

Even if you do not have Shehnaz's patience and forbearance, I think you can learn from her methods and approach. If you approach the intimacy issue with open-mindedness and sincerity, you can create a great and companionable relationship. However if you use the *'Intimacy is my right, and I shall have it'* approach, you're going to make very little progress. You cannot rush emotional togetherness, nor can you demand it. You can only work diligently towards achieving it. Chip away slowly, and a new closeness will emerge. And do try and remember that, when it comes to intimacy and emotional expression, women are far better at it than are men, and therefore, women are well advised to take the lead in ushering true emotional intimacy into the marriage. Needless to say, it would be prudent for the man to follow the woman's lead in this area rather than turning a macho back on it.

12

'Me & My Family' Vs 'You & Your Family'

In my practice as a couples' therapist, I am often surprised to see the number of people accompanying the couples in my waiting room when I open my door. The couple is usually hidden away behind two sets of parents, the person or persons who brought the couple together (if it's an arranged marriage), a few family 'elders' from both sides and maybe, a sibling or two thrown in for good measure. All of them tense and, sometimes, even belligerent. It's almost like the marriage is lost deep inside the family trees.

In such a situation, my first task as a therapist is to identify the couple and get the families out of the marriage space. And let me tell you that this can turn out to be a much more formidable task than it sounds.

After negotiating this minefield, when I finally speak to the couple, I realise they are not as hapless as I originally thought they may be. For, they are as truculent as their respective families are, and have positioned themselves on either sides of a thorny fence. The basic quarrel usually is, '*Me and my family vs you and your family*'.

If you imagine that this sort of scenario happens only in arranged marriages, please stand corrected. Although, in arranged marriages, the families have a greater stake in the union, since they have been actively involved in choosing the partner and organising the wedding, parents of people who chose their own partners can be equally pugnacious and overprotective of their children. As a result, the marriage space (*Chapter 7*) does not get established and both partners tend to be bound to their respective families by rather strong emotional umbilical cords that neither is willing to let go of. For its part, the family too clings on to their respective child's cord either overtly (usually in the case of the man) or covertly (in the case of the woman). When they do this, they end up perpetuating the *my-family- vs- your-family* conflict.

In the past, this particular conflict, though very well known in our country, was never considered as big a deal as it today is. This was largely because everybody accepted it fatalistically as one more reality of life that had to be tolerated. However, as we have discussed earlier, today's couples are not willing to settle for a sub-optimal quality of married life. As a result they actively seek solutions from whatever resources are available in their social environment. Unfortunately, the solutions are not always the right ones.

Kalpana hated her mother-in-law, even though she'd been married to Vidyut for just three weeks. It was an arranged marriage and before the engagement, her mother-in-law had been pleasant enough to her. It was during the engagement that the tensions between the two started. Her father-in-law, never having had a daughter, was very affectionate to Kalpana. Her mother-in-law, on the other hand, went out of her way to be distant to her, constantly complaining about the wedding preparations, the food etc. On the day the couple was to leave for the honeymoon, the mother-in-law had chest pain and palpitations. She had to be hospitalised, the honeymoon was cancelled as a panic-stricken Vidyut wouldn't leave his mother's side, and some of his relatives from out of town were slyly muttering something about the flaws in her horoscope. After being thoroughly investigated, it was established that her mother-in-law's blood pressure had shot up as a result of the stress of the wedding. She pretty much took to bed and was the centre of the household's attention. Kalpana felt her mother-in-law was being dramatic, a sentiment that her new husband, needless to say, did not share. He withdrew from her angrily, even telling his mother what a terrible wife he had. Even her father-in-law was shocked that his daughter-in-law could think along such lines.

Her parents were not much help either, because they had gone to the US to attend the graduation ceremony of Kalpana's brother from business school. Browsing through a glossy in her hairdresser's waiting room, she chanced upon an agony aunt's advice to 'Wretched and Miserable' whose situation seemed similar to her own. The agony aunt's advice was that, to attract her husband's attention, 'Wretched and Miserable' should feign fainting attacks every now and again. Thinking she had nothing to lose, Kalpana proceeded to do just this. Initially, it got her the attention she wanted. But then she tried to do it once too often, and the family doctor, who had initially been sympathetic to her, diagnosed her as suffering from 'hysteria' and recommended psychiatric medication. This precipitated a major family crisis, with Vidyut and his parents accusing of her of being mentally ill and charging her parents of having hidden this fact from them.

Variations of this story take place in love marriages as well. Also, it doesn't make much difference whether the couple is living with the husband's parents or not. In the latter situation, the only saving grace is that the couple have enough private time to work on defining their marriage and individual spaces.

Therefore, such marriages do tend to have an additional safety-net built in, though the net may not fully be in place before problems start cropping up. Often, families and friends get dragged into the tussle and each has their own individual take on the situation. As a result, the couple, rather than coming together to resolve the crisis, end up being polarised. Each sees the other as selfish, uncaring and insensitive. Not the very best of beginnings to a lifelong relationship, don't you think?

Also, it must be said at this point that, adjustment problems with the spouse's family are not the exclusive preserve of women. Being a patriarchal society, more often than not, the woman is expected to leave her childhood home and adopt her husband's family as her own, and progressively over the years, reduce her affiliation with her own family. I am not going to debate the fairness or unfairness of this. This is the reality that we live in, and this is, therefore, the reality that we need to work with. Since the husband is not, by social custom, called upon to adopt his wife's biological family as his own, he obviously faces fewer pressures on this front. If he does forge a healthy relationship with his wife's family, he is considered a god among men, and the woman is considered very fortunate to have found herself such a husband. This does tend to happen with increasing frequency in urban India, for men are certainly far more sensitive today than they used to be, but it can certainly not be considered the norm. Some husbands tend to adopt a patronising attitude towards their parents-in-law, who generally tend to be obsequious towards him and tolerate all his idiosyncrasies, so as not to make their daughters' lives more difficult. In fact, the fuss that is made over the new son-in-law can sometimes appear comical to the unbiased onlooker. The whole system is geared to ensuring that the daughter-in-law is forced to integrate into her husband's family, slowly rejecting her own, however difficult this may be for her. But, (*as we saw in Chapter 4*), the rules are changing in the New Indian Marriage, even if only slowly.

It is, therefore, not uncommon in New Indian Marriages for husbands to find that they too have issues with their parents-in-law. When Ramesh married Leela, after a three-year courtship, he had no idea what was to follow. His father-in-law had great ambitions for Leela and refused to allow something as trivial as marriage to come in the way of his plans. She, on her part, was completely under her father's thumb and went along with everything that he said and did. He, a celebrity cardiac surgeon, took charge of the wedding as well as the marriage. He liked Ramesh, even if he felt the boy lacked the drive to go far. He felt Ramesh's parents were too content and self-contained to give him the necessary impetus.

He used his considerable networking skills and got Ramesh a fast-track job in a leading industrial house and goaded his daughter into obtaining admission for herself in an American Ivy League business school. He insisted she accept the admission, even if this meant that the couple would be separated for a couple of years. He organised things in such a way that Ramesh would be sent on work to the US so he could have 'conjugal visits', as he described it, with Leela. Since his was a larger house than that of Ramesh's parents, he contrived to persuade the couple to live with him and his wife. In fact, he rarely persuaded. He issued diktats and was not used to having them disobeyed. Initially, Ramesh had a good life, but things started going wrong in the marriage, especially on the sexual front. Leela shared this discontent with her mother who, in her customary style, brought this to Leela's father's notice. It was only when he started giving Ramesh sexual advice and handed him a list of websites to visit, and suggested that Ramesh consider surgical implants in his penis, that Ramesh put his foot down and moved out, back to his parents' place. His father-in-law was genuinely bemused by this reaction. He couldn't understand why Ramesh was unwilling to accept the loving help that the older man was offering.

Ramesh's experience is, of course, not really the norm, but I shared it only to highlight the point that husbands too can have serious issues with their in-laws. However, it is more common to see the 'me-and-my-family-vs-you-and-your-family' conflict coalescing around the saas–bahu relationship. Not that this is the only problematic relationship; one can have equally contentious issues with a father-in-law, siblings-in-law or even the spouse's favourite uncle, aunt or cousin. However the saas–bahu relationship bears the brunt of this phase of adjustment and therefore merits greater exploration. (*It must be said that many of the comments in the next section will apply to other family relationships as well, for in the final analysis, in the first year of marriage, any sourness in the relationship with any of one's in-laws is bound to have an adverse impact on defining the marriage space.*)

SAAS AND BAHU—FOUR-LETTER WORDS?

One of the most extraordinary urban developments in recent times is the emergence of the soap opera as a legitimate national addiction. Whatever language your favourite soaps speak in, the contents are pretty much the same. Wicked mother-in-law baits sweet daughter-in-law. Or, as a variation, martyred mother-in-law is harassed by mealy-mouthed daughter-in-law. Every now and again, a dash of a self-centred sister-in-law or a lecherous brother-in-law is thrown in to spice things up. Even a not particularly bright visitor from another planet, chancing upon our soap operas, would have little hesitation in concluding that dowry is no longer the national marital malady, having gracefully ceded centre stage to the saas–bahu power struggle. In fact, this theme has been so over-worked that many mothers-in-law and daughters-in-law who have good and companionable relationships with each other, are looked at askance. And the mothers-in-law of the country are exhorted to remember that *saas bhi kabhi bahu thi* (the mother-in-law was once a daughter-in-law) and the nation's daughters-in-law are expected to comfort themselves with the thought that *bahu bhi kabhi saas banegi* (the daughter-in-law will one day be a mother-in-law).

Conventional wisdom has it that the difficulty in the saas–bahu equation lies in the inability of the two protagonists to work out a time-share arrangement regarding the man in their lives. In fact, a recent conversation I had with a slightly older lady, who attended one of my talks on marriage, is quite revealing. The lady in question accosted me, in the company of a few other ladies, of whom she was evidently the anointed spokesperson. Our conversation went something like this:

'You are too sympathetic to the daughter-in-law,' she began, without preamble.

'Really?' was the best I could muster.

'Then what! You don't understand the mother-in-law's point of view at all.'

'What is that?' I asked, entering the road she was intent on leading me down.

'See. I am the boy's mother. I have brought him up for 25 years. Why should I give him up to a chit of a girl?'

I tried to reason that her son was not a commodity that was up for barter.

'Of course, he isn't,' she snapped. 'He is my son, after all.'

We weren't getting anywhere. I tried a different tack. I tried telling her that statistically a man spends a larger chunk of his life with his wife than with his mother, and that maybe this was the reason her daughter-in-law expected to be given priority. I had played into her hands.

'Exactly!' she said. 'She's going to have my son for the rest of her life. Why can't I have him while I am still alive?'

I again brought up the son—commodity issue. She harrumphed her way out of that.

'But what does your son feel about this?' I asked.

'Poor boy! What can he do? He's getting blood pressure now,' she said sadly.

The conversation flagged as all of us silently commiserated on her absent son's hypertensive problems. Then she became placatory.

'See, I am not saying that she cannot have my son. Let her take him. But not so soon. Within fifteen days of marriage she wants him entirely to herself. Can't she wait for a decent interval?' she demanded.

I dared not ask, but anyway did. 'What is a decent interval?'

'Five years, at least,' she said, like she had given the subject some serious thought. The other women nodded their heads vigorously and made loud assenting noises as if they found this a perfectly reasonable time-frame for the conveyance of ownership. The expression on my face, as I marshalled my thoughts for an appropriate response, seemed to put her on the back foot.

She said, with a glance at her sisters-in-arms, 'Okay if you think five years is too much, what about three years?' Evidently, one or two of the others didn't entirely like her backing down so much and I heard muttered expressions that sounded like 'at least four years', but they didn't push it.

'But this is like bargaining for brinjals,' I expostulated.

By now, our discussion had attracted the attention of some of the others and slowly the group was becoming bigger. And what was more, younger women were joining the group. The spokesperson seemed to realise this, for she was getting more edgy.

'Three years is the minimum requirement,' she said with finality, and turning her back to me, walked away with all the dignity and grace she could muster, which was not inconsiderable. Her sisters-in-arms melted away.

This conversation had quite an impact on me, for I did not view it using conventional wisdom as my framework. Yes, it did tell me that the older lady was feeling threatened by the pre-eminence her daughter-in-law was obviously being accorded in her son's life.

And on the surface, one can explain away her demand as a clamour for ownership. But the issue goes much deeper than this. For if you notice, it is not the kind of person her daughter-in-law was that the lady had a problem with. It was merely the fact that *the daughter-in-law was taking her son away*, that caused the older lady pain. Had not the son been a bone of contention, it was even conceivable that the two women would have got along at least reasonably, if not well. How often have we seen a younger woman getting along famously with an older woman—until she ends up marrying the latter's son? Often, the period of engagement is even a bit of a honeymoon between a woman and her fiancé's mother. For this is the time when they are genuinely getting to know each other without any preconceived expectations of each other. But once the wedding's over, everything changes. And dramatically, at that.

As I said earlier, it was not the daughter-in-law's traits that made my interlocutor unhappy. It was the fact that her son was not sensitive enough to her needs as a mother. Obviously, the couple was recently married. A few more months of this and the mother-in-law's ire would doubtless get transferred onto her daughter-in-law, since she could not sustain any degree of hostility against her son. The point I am trying to make is that the *saas-bahu problem is not really a question of two women not being able to get along*. It is just that, often, they get off on pretty much the wrong foot simply because the template of their relationship is so poorly defined.

Most relationships are purposeful, but the only reason the saas and bahu come together is because of the common man in their lives. The woman needs her man; she needs her parents; she needs her siblings; she needs her friends; but she can well do without a mother-in-law. She can choose her husband, but she can't choose her mother-in-law, who comes as part of the overall package. From the mother's point of view, she can mould and has moulded her son, but the daughter-in-law comes from a different mould. As a result, saas and bahu do not find the opportunity or occasion to get to know each other, woman to woman, human being to human being, person to person. And the template for their relationship—and this seems culturally almost pre-ordained—is adversarial and not mutually respectful. So who is the four-letter word? Saas? Bahu? Or Pati?

As I see it, there are three important reasons why many, though not all, saas–bahu relationships get stuck in this fateful template:

The first and most important of these lies in the mother–son relationship. When mothers and grown-up sons have not moved their relationships to the adult plane, the only way they can express their love and concern for each other is through childhood patterns: the mother gives, the son takes. And when the mother finds her son taking from somewhere else, she inevitably feels threatened.

The second has its origins in the husband–wife relationship itself. Obviously, the marriage space (*Chapter 7*) takes some time to get defined and in the interim period, both partners have not yet agreed upon parameters with which to respond to the mother/saas. So the man expects his wife to love his mother as he does (an unworkable expectation). Naturally, fireworks are the inevitable result. I am not saying one cannot love one's mother-in-law. One most certainly can, and I know several people who do. However to *expect* one's partner to do so is not being particularly fair on the partner.

And the third reason lies in the bahu's relationship with her own mother. When she finds the relationship with her saas floundering, many a bahu tends to displace, unconsciously of course, a lot of the emotional baggage from the mother–daughter relationship on to the saas–bahu relationship. After all, thinking of the saas as wicked is fine, but whoever heard of one's own mother being the bane of one's life?

Is it then ever possible for saas and bahu to overcome the four-letter handicap and have a companionable relationship with each other? There most certainly is. Read on.

WE AND OUR FAMILIES

The only way to substantially deal with the *me-and-my-family-vs-you-and-your-family* conflict is to get to the point where the couple think more in terms of

'*We and Our Families*'. In other words, we need to think of the marriage (We) as the primary unit, and see this unit (both partners together) dealing with the needs of both sets of families. It is no longer a question of the wife rejecting her family and adopting her husband's family as her own, or the husband being swallowed up by the wife's family. The New Indian Marriage demands that couples define their mutually comfortable marriage space and create their own marriage templates (*Chapter 8*). This implies that once the marriage space gets defined, the couple needs to *establish boundaries between the marriage space and the family space,* thereby making the marriage space sacrosanct, inviolable and inaccessible to anybody other than both the partners; and this includes parents, siblings and other family members. Try and think of it as creating a protective bubble around your marriage—*the marriage bubble.* Many couples have successfully used the following guidelines to arrive at the *We-and-Our-Families* resolution.

Marriage is between two individuals and not two families

The protagonists of the joint-family system tend to believe that marriage is between two families and not two individuals. As a result, at weddings, the bridal couple are usually incidental to the proceedings. The big fat Indian wedding is designed to provide bonding opportunities for both sets of extended families and friends. However, as is well known, the bride's family plays host to the event and is generally seen as fair game to be trampled upon by the bridegroom's family. So, instead of bonding, gaps start opening up between the families, and if these are not adequately managed, they can sometimes end up in overt hostility.

Needless to say, the bridal couple feels the impact of all of this much later, when the gossip mills start to grind. And in the first years of the marriage, communication between families is kept alive through the practice of age-old rituals that made perfect sense in the times they were conceived, but are impractical in today's life. As many occasions as are possible are created for the families to meet, share a meal and so on. In general, family members have no compunctions in making inroads into the marriage. Fortunately, the New Indian Marriage has changed things around, and more couples today treat marriage as a union between two individuals and not two families. If both sets of families get along, it is a nice bonus, but this is not the primary focus of the marriage.

Parents can be irrational

Our parents are good, but fallible, human beings. This means they can get irrational every now and again and therefore, are not always right in whatever they say and do. The funny thing is that most people feel this way, sometimes even more strongly, about their parents before they get married, but once they are married, they refuse to see any of their parents' shortcomings, particularly when these are pointed out by their partners. This usually happens because in the newly-married state, as one starts realising the gravity of the marital role and gets in touch with the fact that one's life has changed forever, one feels vulnerable and helpless, like a child. One's spouse has not yet become a companion and so one tends to fall back on the people whom one has been more familiar with—one's parents.

Akhil had a very difficult relationship with his parents through his teenage and young adult years. His parents were more focussed on their social lives and dealing with his sister's marital problems. He thought of them as selfish, inconsiderate and unloving, and he shared his feelings regarding his family, with everyone who would listen to him, including Rebecca, his girlfriend, whom he eventually married. During the wedding a subtle shift seemed to take place in his relationship with his parents. They started treating him more like an adult and he started feeling closer to them. Rebecca had a reasonable equation with them, but she kept her distance because of everything she'd heard about them from Akhil. A couple of weeks after they returned from their honeymoon, she made some snide remark about his mother and he exploded.

'Say anything you want about me, but don't say a word against my family!'

This is a fairly common response, more on the part of the man, but also on the part of the woman, in the early stages of the marriage. When you look at the statement, the underlying implication is that one wants to protect one's family from the partner. Why do we need to do this? Will the presence of a new element threaten the integrity of the family? If it indeed does, obviously the family was never close in the first place, right? Also, the implication in this statement is, 'I still belong to my family and you are the outsider', hardly a great way to help someone integrate into your family. So next time you hear yourself thinking or saying these words, bite your tongue and remember that your parents can be irrational people, as you well know, and that you want your partner to have a comfortable equation with your family and not feel alienated from them.

You are not letting down your family if you agree with your partner's critique of them

The primary reason for not talking about one's family's foibles is the fear that, if one does so, one would be letting them down in front of one's partner. Absolutely untrue. Whomever you have a relationship with, you are going to have some issues. This is the hallmark of all relationships, whether it is with your partner, parents, siblings or friends. And when you do come face to face with some irritating behaviour that any of your family members have displayed, the safest place to let off steam is in the privacy of your marital relationship. Your fear is that your partner may pass judgement on your family members if you come up with too many negative feelings. If you discuss this with your partner up front, both of you may be able to clear the air and establish an understanding that merely because one is critical of one's family does not mean that one does not love them. You're not letting your family down when you discuss them with your partner, you're only letting your partner come closer to you. Don't feel that by sharing things about your family, you're giving your partner control over you. You're not.

Is 'going nuclear' a better option?

Not always. If this were the case, couples living in other cities or even countries, would have a much better quality of married life. It is not geographical distance away from the family that matters, it's what's in your mind that does. Rajendran and Malar went to Dubai almost immediately after they got married. Malar's family thought this was a godsend, for their daughter could concentrate on establishing her marriage without the distraction of having to deal with in-laws. They couldn't have been further from the truth. Not that Rajendran ill-treated Malar. On the contrary, he was very affectionate and looked after her needs very well. The only problem was that he expected Malar to speak to his mother every day and report on everything they were doing. Her mother-in-law remote-controlled their lives from India. In case Malar 'forgot' to call, Rajendran would know (for he would call his mother independently from work every day to check whether Malar had called her), and they would have a big row.

This notwithstanding, I believe that as a rule of thumb, *a few years in a nuclear family lifestyle is very desirable for a couple, even if their parents live in the same city* . Not to get away from the family, but to learn the mechanics of independent living. I have found several couples who always lived with the husband's parents, having terrible adjustment problems when the parents passed on, because even as adults they lived under the parents' umbrella and had a hard time learning to take independent decisions without their parents' approval. Of course, whether or not you can live independently will be determined by factors such as economics, sub-cultural dynamics, state of parents' health, and the like. But if it is possible, I think it's a very useful thing to do. Increasingly, in urban India, parents don't seem to mind if their married children create their own independent homes in the same city. One doesn't any more have to seek a transfer or find a job in another city, just to have one's own home.

Cut your emotional umbilical cord

Finally, this is what needs to be done to define and establish the marriage bubble. Most of us in India, even after we reach adulthood, remain connected to our parents by an emotional umbilical cord. You may remember that the umbilical cord, by which the growing foetus is connected to the mother's uterus, is the primary source of the foetus' survival, for it is only through the cord that the foetus obtains all its nutritional requirements. When the child is born, the umbilical cord is cut, so that the child can function as an independent entity. Likewise, our emotional umbilical cord, by which we are connected to our parents to help us function in our social environments until we are ready to do so alone, also needs to be cut, to enable us to function as independent adults.

When I say the cord needs to be cut, I am not at all suggesting that we cut off from our parents. What I am saying is that we move our relationship with our parents to a more adult plane. We stop being over-dependent on them. We don't expect their protection any more. We start taking major decisions for ourselves without feeling compelled to accept all the advice they give. We don't shut them out of our lives; we just enrich our relationship by becoming adults. However to do this, one basic hurdle needs to be overcome: the fear on the part of both parent and offspring, that if the cord is cut, whatever relationship exists may be permanently damaged. Or put another way, 'we have no idea how else we can relate to each other'.

While this fear is entirely understandable, it is without real basis. I have seen far too many families successfully making the effort, to believe otherwise. I have seen stentorian septuagenarians 'letting go' of their children, as well as 'dutiful children' cutting their cords effectively. And when we finally cut our cords and emerge from our chrysalis as mature adults, we find that we are able to define a boundary between our marriage space and our family space, thereby getting the best out of both the spaces. And do remember that cutting the cord is something that both partners need to do. Women do tend to believe that by virtue of having come away from their parental homes, they have cut their cords. Not true. As I've said earlier, it's not physical or geographical distance that matters, it's the undue influence these connections have inside your head that does.

SOME THINGS THE HUSBAND NEEDS TO REMEMBER

Don't expect your wife to love your parents as you do

I can't tell you how many men in our country expect that their wives will love their parents as they do. And if the wife doesn't seem to comply, they get aggressive with her. The standard argument that's offered is a variation of this: 'I am what I am because of my parents. They have sacrificed so much for my sake and have brought me up to be what I am. No other parent would have done this much for their children.' Let's get something clear, gentlemen. This is what all children feel about their parents. All parents make sacrifices for their children; it's pretty much part of their job description. I know you feel grateful for everything your parents did for you and I believe you have every reason to be. In your eyes, they are the best parents in the world. But you can't reasonably expect other people who have not been at the receiving end of their love, attention and sacrifice for more than two decades to feel as you do. Can you love her parents as you love your own? Of course, you can't. They're not your parents. Likewise, it's unfair to expect your wife to love your parents the way you do. What you certainly can expect is that your wife be nice to your parents. And that if she experiences any discomfort with them, to discuss it with you first, rather than take matters into her own hands. But anything more than this would be asking for too much.

When she complains to you about your parents, don't take it personally

As we have discussed before, parents can, every now and again, be irrational and difficult to handle. Since your transactions with them are limited, you might not realise this, but your wife is expected to interact with them more and she is, therefore, more likely to be at the receiving end of their irrationalities than you are. And this applies to working wives too, for soon after you get married, you'll find that your parents start communicating more with your wife than with you. Usually, when they want to take you to task over something, they end up taking her to task instead. So, when she complains about this, don't personalise it and fly off the handle. *'How dare you say anything against my parents?'* does not help. She needs a vent to let off some steam and if you don't provide her that outlet, she's going to have to do so to her parents or friends. And you're not going to like that. At the beginning, she doesn't have any ill-will against your parents. Why should she? But if she doesn't have your ear, ill-will can develop.

Don't feel compelled to provide solutions each time she lets off steam

When your wife cribs about something your parents did, said or did not say or do, you don't always have to jump in with a solution. There are some problems that don't have an immediate solution and there are some that do. If each time your wife complains about your mother, you are going to call a family meeting and try and thrash out a solution, your family life is in for some very troubled times, and your wife's relationship with your mother is never going to happen. What is needed is a supportive approach with your wife. If you hear her out sympathetically, half her problem is solved. After this, if both of you can discuss strategies to deal with this, you'll definitely find a way to deal with the issue. There will be some things that you'll have to do and some things that she will. End result: a workable joint strategy that not only solves the problem but also brings the two of you closer together.

Don't get defensive of your family members

This is something that guys routinely do when they try to smoothen out an unpleasant situation. When Rebecca came home from a shopping expedition with her sister-in-law, she was furious. Her sister-in-law, who was based in the US and in town on vacation, had insisted on choosing all the clothes at the boutique they went to and shot down everything that Rebecca had liked. Of course, her sister-in-law had paid for the clothes, but Rebecca was now stuck with three outfits she was not particularly crazy about, because they were old-fashioned and covered every part of her anatomy, even those she didn't want to cover. When Akhil came home, she ranted about her perception that her sister-in-law was trying to suggest that Rebecca needed to dress more modestly. Akhil listened for a while because he was in a good mood, and eventually told her that she was over-reacting (women hate to hear that word!). He also said that his sister was a person of impeccable taste and that when she was trying to suggest something, Rebecca should listen and so on. Akhil thought he'd handled the situation very well (mainly because he didn't explode), and was therefore very surprised that Rebecca got really upset with him.

When Akhil was trying to explain away his sister's behaviour, he was actually being defensive of her. Also, he was unwilling to appreciate that Rebecca could have a point about his sister wanting Rebecca to dress more modestly. And he was expecting Rebecca, who was at the receiving end of what she perceived as her sister-in-law's irrationality, to take the larger view and not misinterpret what he perceived as her 'good intentions'. When a wife shares her perceptions of his family, a man would do well to stop being defensive of his parents and siblings. Then he can actually stand to learn a good deal more about them than he otherwise would have. Often, though not all the time, the wife's perception is reasonably accurate, simply because, by virtue of trying to establish herself in her new family, her antennae are very finely tuned to discordant notes in her environment.

Stand up for your wife

This is one of the biggest difficulties that many women have with their husbands. When it comes to any kind of communication difficulties with his family, the men stand back and accept meekly whatever the family members say, and don't stand up for the wife. I'm not suggesting that the man should defend any indefensible deeds or words of the wife, or argue on her behalf over petty things. The position he would be well advised to take is to get his family to cut his wife some slack and try and understand the difficult position she is in. What the husband fears is that his family members will think that he is giving his wife more importance, and this offends his sense of machismo. However, it needs to be remembered that the wife is making most of the adjustments and if she falters every now and again, this should not be held against her.

If the other family members get a little upset, don't worry about it. They'll get over it sooner than later. But if they see that the husband is solidly behind the wife, they will be less inclined to take her to task for every little thing that goes wrong. Your family will always be with you. But to get your wife to be accepted by your family, your support is critical, even if there are a few hits and misses along the way. If you want to say something negative to your wife, do so in the privacy of your bedroom, don't give her a dressing-down in everybody else's presence.

Don't expect your wife to 'fight her battles' on her own

It is not uncommon for men to say that it's the wife's responsibility to establish herself in his family. She simply cannot do this without your support and participation. Yes, the initial year may be a little difficult for the man as he tries to do a balancing act between wife and family, but if he communicates to his wife that he will work with her on this, the balancing act will soon become unnecessary. Keep up the teetering and you'll soon fall flat on your face. End result: neither your wife nor your family is going to be pleased with you.

Include your wife in family decisions

When Rajashri got married and came to live with Rajan's family, she was full of beans and bonhomie. She was working and had independent savings of her own. When she realised that the refrigerator in her new family home was giving trouble, she offered to buy a new one. Rajan, his parents and his brother went out shopping for one and picked up the latest model of refrigerator in the market. She was neither consulted on the budget nor the model to buy, and was expected only to make the payment. Naturally, she was upset. The only way your wife can feel part of your family is if she's part of the decision-making process. If everything is left to the elders or to the men in the family, she's hardly going to be integrated, is she?

Don't confuse the marriage space with the family space

When a bride enters the home, the parents expect to be involved in a lot of things the couple do. Some areas of these may be acceptable, because they are legitimately in the family domain and involve some input from other family members—such as buying a new vehicle or whether or not to attend a distant relative's wedding. However, if she has to end up taking your parents' permission to have a cup of coffee with her friends, or both of you have to take permission to go to the movies, some amount of resentment is bound to crop up. Also, whatever happens in your marriage space should never be shared with family members. Both of you need to decide what level of privacy you'd like to operate at, and work within that framework. If your parents are going to tell you how to conduct your marriage, you are bound to have a problem.

Rajan's mother did not like the idea of the couple locking their bedroom door when they were inside, for she felt it was rude. Rajan complied with her wishes, and the end result was a hurried and uncomfortable sex life. His mother was also very unhappy that Rajashri locked her cupboard door and took the keys with her when she went out of the house, something that she had done even in her parent's house. Her mother-in-law felt that she was not being trusted. Rajashri had reason to lock her cupboard because she was positive, although she had no evidence, that on one occasion, when she had left the cupboard unlocked, the older lady had rifled through its contents. Naturally, she could say nothing. I'm not suggesting that all mothers-in-law are like this, but the bottom line is that both partners should firmly enforce the level of privacy they both want.

Another common mistake is to involve the whole family in a marital fight. Living in apartments as most of us do, it is likely that the other family members may be aware when the couple is fighting. If they insist on getting involved and giving their opinion, it should be made clear to them that while both of you appreciate their concern, there are some things that both of you have to learn to sort out on your own.

Respect her relationship with her family and build your own relationship with them

Some men, by virtue of sub-cultural conditioning, tend to have a mocking attitude towards their wife's family. Nothing will alienate the wife more than this. Rajan had little respect for Rajashri's father and he made no bones about showing this. She did not entirely disagree with her husband, for she too had ongoing issues with her father. But when his whole family started making scoffing statements about her father, she saw red, because she felt that it was

Rajan's attitude that encouraged his family to be negatively disposed towards her father. Certainly, her family were bound to have imperfections and idiosyncrasies. But this did not mean that she didn't love them. You need to remember that, just as you expect your wife to be nice to your family, so must you, too, reciprocate.

There is another widespread practice when a woman gets married to a man who's based overseas or in another city, that in the interim period, while she's awaiting her visa or transfer, she should live with and look after his parents and not her own. It's hard enough for a newlywed wife to be separated from her husband for long periods; it's even more difficult if she has to start an adjustment process with her in-laws on her own, without her husband's presence. Now, if she could choose where to stay during the transition, that would help tremendously. I have found that when given such a choice, most women tend to divide their time equally between their parents and parents-in-law. It gives her a feeling that her family is also respected. You might also want to consider participating more in her family's life, instead of confining your involvement to weekly lunch or dinner visits, and occasional bored telephone conversations.

SOME THINGS THE WIFE WOULD DO WELL TO REMEMBER

Don't feel compelled to love your parents-in-law

Shortly after the wedding, when the whole family seems to be basking in a bit of a glow, there is usually the tendency for a few speeches to be made by everybody in the family. It's possible you may be subject to the 'I-have-not-lost-a-son-but-gained-a-daughter' spiel. Don't take this literally. For you might then be tempted to expect your parents-in-law to treat you like a daughter. If things work out well, this might actually happen, but don't *expect* it to—and feel disappointed when it doesn't. By the same token, you don't have to love them like you do your parents. But, by taking things slowly, you have a better chance of establishing long-term peace. Like all other relationships, family relationships too need time to be nurtured and developed. However, many women, with the best of intentions, try the 'all-or-none' approach, and find they fall flat on their faces. Aim first for a civil relationship and *then* for a working relationship. The loving relationship will then follow. Many young brides make the mistake of trying to trade in their family for their husband's. Never works. Your mother-in-law is your mother-in-law, not your mother. Your brother-in-law is your brother-in-law, not your brother, and so on.

Don't try and reach your husband through his family

Many a young bride has tried to earn brownie points with her husband by being dutiful and loving to his family. This is extremely hard to sustain. It's important that your husband's family feels that whatever you do for them, you do because you want to, and not because you feel that the best way to your husband's heart is through his family. Sundari did just this when she married Prakash. During the engagement period he had told her that he had only one expectation of her: that she should look after his mother and younger sister. Other than this, she could pretty much do what she pleased. He was a generally serious sort of chap who worked hard and kept to himself. He wasn't a sparkling conversationalist, but he was a solid and dependable person, which she was grateful for, since these were the exact qualities that her father lacked. She determined she would win him over by taking such good care of his family that he would have no option but to see what a sterling woman he'd married.

She set about her task like a woman possessed. Her mother-in-law and sister-in-law were pampered and even smothered. Prakash was quite pleased about this, though he didn't show it, for he was not that kind of guy. Sooner than later, the bubble had to burst, and it did. One day, exhausted by her efforts, she burst into tears. Her mother-in-law tried to console her and find out the reason for her unhappiness. In the course of the ensuing conversation, Sundari artlessly told her that despite everything she was doing for the family, Prakash was so unappreciative of her. She went on to wonder whether anything she did made any difference to him. Naturally, the mother-in-law was upset. She accused Sundari of being a sham and a manipulator. Her sister-in-law felt betrayed, and Prakash withdrew even more from her. It took a long time for everyone to recover from this false start.

Respect your mother-in-law's needs and insecurities, but define boundaries all the same

As we have discussed, your mother-in-law is going to feel threatened just a tad by your presence, however easy-going you may be. This, as we have seen, has nothing to do with you, but has more to do with your husband's relationship with her. So don't take it personally if she tends to throw rank every now and again. She's really sending out a signal to your husband when she does this. Try and get your husband to respond to her signal. However, if you find that your mother-in-law tends to overuse you as her route of communication with her son, you do need to define your boundaries with her. You can do this without causing offence to her by gently, though firmly, getting the message across to her as to how far she can go with you. You have done this with your friends, maybe with your parents and maybe even with your husband. Now's the time to do the same with your mother-in-law as well. If you approach this task with understanding and the genuine desire to retain a relationship with her, you'll find that she's able to pick up the sincerity of your effort and will respond accordingly.

Talk to your husband about his family, but don't get judgemental

If something they say or do maddens or upsets you, talk to your husband about it. Don't get into the mindset that you shouldn't bother him with trivia or that he might get upset. Dealing with his family is not a trivial matter and both of you need to learn to do it together. Even as you attempt to define your boundaries with your in-laws, you do need your husband's support in this effort. You therefore need to learn to share with your husband your thoughts and feelings about them, without putting him on the defensive. Remember, he's seen all the soap operas as well and will tend to get all edgy and protective of his mother if you put him on the back foot. On the other hand, if you get the message across to him that you do intend to have a relationship with his mother even if it kills you, you'll find he becomes your ally. However, try not to get killed in the process. Likewise, don't fly off the handle if he finds your family quirky.

Give him an opportunity to tell you if and how your family members get under his skin. It will make him more amenable to lending you an ear if you reciprocate.

Don't bend over backwards and regret it later

To be accepted by his family, don't try too hard to be accepted. Paradoxical as this may sound, this could happen. The harder you try and the more you bend over backwards, the less likely you are to be accepted, for when you do all of this, you end up behaving unnaturally, will be unable to sustain the effort for too long and worse still, end up full of resentment. Just try and be yourself. Many fights begin with 'I've bent over backwards to please them and they don't appreciate it.' Why should they? They didn't ask you to bend over backwards, did they? You did this of your own volition. So, there's no point feeling resentful that you did. The better thing to do would be to determine precisely how much you can accommodate your in-laws and extend yourself only as much as you are capable of doing.

Zarina was absolutely delighted with her parents-in-law. They were much more liberated and progressive in their thinking than her parents, and Zarina had much more freedom in the kind of lifestyle she chose to lead. She felt the need to reciprocate and did their every bidding, even anticipating their needs and fetching and carrying for them, like a grateful puppy. Her parents-in-law were a bit taken aback initially, but soon got used to their daughter-in-law's attentiveness. Not surprisingly, Zaheer, her husband, was ecstatic with this turn of events. Soon, Zarina had structured a lifestyle where she had hardly any time for herself, always doing things for her parents-in-law or her husband. She hated visiting her parental home, for she felt so out of place there. Even her cousins and old friends seemed provincial and small-minded in their thinking, and she found her conversations with them full of long and uncomfortable pauses.

So, she put even more energy into looking after her husband's family, extended family and friends. Soon, she started finding it physically more and more difficult to keep the pace going. She had migraines, body aches, frequent bouts of fever and a general feeling of lassitude. The doctor said nothing was really wrong with her, but her energy and zeal were flagging. By now, her in-laws, used to a new standard of being looked after, felt that she was neglecting them, and frequent scenes would ensue. All the camaraderie and joie de vivre of the first few months had been replaced by a feeling of general sulkiness and ill humour. Zarina couldn't understand why her parents-in-law were being so difficult when she had bent over backwards to look after them. And they couldn't understand why she was peeved with them, for they had not asked her to do anything, had they?

Don't displace emotions on your mother-in-law from other relationships

Often, we have unfulfilled expectations of our own parents, which we may find difficult to discuss with them. However, displacing these expectations on your mother-in-law is not fair on the latter. Typically, many women end up getting married to get away from an oppressive atmosphere at home. In this case, they expect that the ambience in their new home will compensate for whatever they have missed earlier. And since the mother-in-law is the centre of the new home, most expectations fall on her shoulders.

These, like expecting your mother-in-law to be the mother you never had, are unrealistic expectations. She has her limitations and can only function within them. *You know that you are displacing expectations when you find that many of the things about your mother-in-law that make you mad are the same things that upset you about your mother.* Also, just like men tend to blame most of their wives' irrationalities on PMS, women tend to blame their husband's insensitivities on their mothers-in-law, believing the latter were over-indulgent of their sons' foibles. While there could be a grain of truth to these feelings, PMS and mothers-in-law have had to shoulder more than their fair share of blame in contemporary life. Try not to fall into this trap.

Get your husband to accept and be accepted by your family

Remember, you're dealing with two families. So don't ignore your own. Try and get your husband to participate in your family's activities as well. If he's reluctant, coax him. Going quid pro quo in the business of dealing with families is perfectly acceptable.

Allow them to get to know you, warts and all, but don't get drawn into his family's politics

Being accepted by his family means that they get to know you as you are, not as what they want you to be. So don't be wary of showing them your imperfections. This way, the relationship can be a honest one. Bust the 'ideal daughter-in-law' myth once and for all from your mind and theirs. All families are political units, so politics is bound to exist. The arrival of a new person usually sets off the processes of wooing her to one side or another. Bear this in mind, enjoy the wooing while it lasts, but don't take sides.

Above all, remember his family is an add-on to your marriage and not its epicentre

It's your own marriage that should be the centre of your family life. If you define what we have discussed as the 'marriage bubble' well, you'll find that you and your husband can together deal with anything that you come up against.

If you pay some attention to defining your 'We space', defining boundaries between the marriage and the family, using the guidelines described above, should not be difficult. I'm not suggesting that it'll be a breeze, for there is certainly effort required of both partners, but it need not be as soul-searing and heart-wrenching as contemporary soap operas would have us believe.

13

Work Hard, Party Hard

'I work hard. I party hard. Hope you do too!' Not by any means, the most romantic of opening lines, but on less impressive starts have long-term relationships begun. For reasons she is still hard-pressed to understand, Rashmi found this opening line thrown casually her way by Amar at their favourite pub, absolutely irresistible. It gave her the feeling that they were soulmates for she felt the same way about life too: enjoy it while you can and the future would take care of itself. Both of them worked in the BPO sector and lived what could be called 'jet-lagged' lives. Conference calls through the night, sleeping through the day, socialising when they could, earning salaries their parents never dreamt of. All in all, both were happy with their choice of jobs. Along the way, they got married and continued partying hard and working hard. Soon, Amar's hard work was appreciated by his bosses and he was rewarded with a senior management position, which meant he had to work harder and travel a bit. So, while both of them still partied hard, they had to do so independently, sometimes in different cities, because their schedules could not always be harmonised.

You don't have to be a rocket scientist to figure out what happened next. Amar had a few one-night stands with business colleagues—'nothing serious. Just to relieve the monotony'. Independently, Rashmi was getting emotionally dependent on Varun, one of their mutual friends, but hadn't actually gone to bed with him. When she found out about Amar's peccadilloes, she took her relationship with Varun to the next level. When she told Amar that she was in love with Varun and wanted a divorce, her husband was livid. Despite his apparent liberal lifestyle, he was essentially conservative, and believed that it was not acceptable for a woman to 'stray' in her marriage. He became belligerent, got into drunken brawls with Varun at the pub and other public places, and refused to consent to a divorce. He escalated matters to their parents and the whole situation became one big mess.

When you work hard and party hard, what basically happens is that you prioritise your work and your social life over your marriage. You don't need me to tell you how it'll end, do you? Between work and friends, I would say that work can create a more adverse impact on marriage, if its place is not clearly defined in your life. The reason is that work has today come to occupy a central position in our lives. We tend to define our identity through the work we do and derive our self-esteem from what our bosses and peers at work think of us. We tend to think of ourselves first as bankers, deejays, managers, doctors or software engineers, and only then as men or women, and finally as husband, wife, sibling, friend or child. All our emotional energies are directed towards our work, where we are obsessed with excellence; whatever dregs we can spare, we scatter tiredly around our personal relationships. Work dominates our thinking, whether we are at work or at home. And if our partner feels and does the same, we consider ourselves lucky that there's no nagging to deal with.

However, not all partners feel the same way and this is where the problems begin. How much time and energy are you going to allocate to the work domain? The commonest response to this question is, 'I'm not in control of that. It's the work culture. If I don't work as hard as I do, I'll be out of a job'. Just look at yourself in the mirror, be honest with yourself and tell me that's really true. If you're being absolutely truthful, you would say that you actually enjoy working as hard as you do. You enjoy the time you spend with colleagues. You enjoy the buzz of a job well completed. You enjoy the accolades you receive at work. You enjoy the challenges your boss places in front of you. You enjoy grinding a disliked colleague to pulp. You're having a whole lot of fun.

And when you're doing all this, the last person on your mind is your spouse. And when your spouse remonstrates with you, your standard response, if you're a man, is, 'But I'm doing this for you and the family', and if you're a woman, 'But, you don't complain about the money I'm bringing in. This is the price we have to pay', or variations along that theme. These effectively shut the spouse up and life goes on. Until the next crisis hits. Or until one or both of you ends up a workaholic. Or one or both of you suffers from *early burnout syndrome*. There is, of course, another option: just like you defined a boundary between your marriage space and your family space (*Chapter 12*), you might consider doing the same between your marriage space and work space, and between your marriage space and your recreational space.

WORK BOUNDARIES

The physical environment in today's offices, particularly some of the more recent and upmarket ones, has become increasingly attractive to employees. A lot of attention is paid to beautifying the space one works in. Office cafeterias aren't the grubby places they used to be. You might even have a gymnasium and a swimming pool for you to work out in after you've been worked up by office frustrations. And overall, the work culture itself tends to breed overwork: contemporary work culture demands a punishing 80-plus-hours-a-week schedule. As a result of all this, many couples seem to gravitate away from each other and towards work. And if you're living in a metropolis, the travails of commuting ensure even less time for family and other pursuits.

However, given the fact that you're newly married, you do need to appreciate that your marriage needs your attention, if the foundations are to be laid well. For this to happen, you need to define the boundaries between your work space and marriage space. The general principles of boundary definition (*described in Chapter 10*) apply in this situation as well. For convenience, let us recapitulate some of the salient features of boundaries.

1. A boundary is an imaginary line telling us how much we are prepared to extend ourselves for an individual or a domain. In this situation, it would refer to how much we are prepared to permit or accommodate the work domain to encroach upon our marriage space. While I do appreciate that work can be very demanding and today's work culture requires us to extend ourselves substantially if we are to experience professional growth, the problems start only when we bend over backwards in our work domain and allow it to intrude too much into our marriage space, thereby denying ourselves

the opportunity to build a substantial enough platform for our personal lives.

2. *There are no right and wrong boundaries, only congruent and incongruent ones.* If both partners are comfortable with a boundary, it becomes congruent and poses no problem. Since Rashmi and Amar were initially perfectly comfortable with the 'work-hard-party-hard' dynamic, a congruent boundary can be said to have existed. However, the boundaries soon became incongruent when neither was comfortable with what the other was doing in their respective work and friendship domains, and the problems started. Do remember that even if something is working for you and both of you are genuinely comfortable with it, if enough time and energy is not invested in the marriage space, things are bound to become difficult. There is, of course, no such thing as a formula for how much you can allow work to invade your personal life, but if you find that either one or both of you feel unfulfilled or unhappy with the state of affairs, a case exists for boundary revision.

3. *Boundaries can be tight or relaxed.* People who, for whatever reason, need to spend more time at work than others, generally tend to draw their work boundaries very close and very tightly around themselves. In other words,

they are very possessive about their work domain and don't like it at all when the partner tries to infiltrate it. Some of us think of ourselves as workaholics and wear this as a badge of honour. Believe me, being a workaholic is nothing to be proud of; sooner than later you will burn out. The problem with workaholism is that you derive your identity almost entirely from your work space. This makes you extremely vulnerable, for when things start going wrong at work, as they invariably do every now and again, you are at a high risk for crashing into an early burnout situation. However, if you derive your identity from something more substantial, like your personal relationships, and see your work space as a platform that provides you the opportunity to strive for excellence and a good quality of life, you become less vulnerable. As partners get more comfortable with each other, tight boundaries will progressively loosen and eventually relax.

4. *Boundaries change with time.* Our boundaries are not carved in stone; they are always changing. So one need not worry that the boundaries that exist in the beginning of a marriage will remain for the rest of one's married life. This applies to relaxed as well as tight boundaries. At different stages of your life, you may find

that the work domain requires greater investment of time and energy and a hitherto loose boundary may become slightly tighter. But this need not be a problem if both partners respect this and give each other space and time to loosen the boundary again.

When Anirudh and Shirley got married, they were relatively junior in their respective jobs and were able to give each other a lot of time. However, within six months of their wedding, Anirudh got a promotion that demanded he spend more time away from home, travelling to different parts of the country. While both were happy that he was growing professionally and was also being paid very well for his efforts, both were unhappy with the lack of time for each other. They talked about it and decided that both would work really hard for the next year or two, save some money, and then see if they could change their jobs to less demanding ones. Shirley requested for and obtained an assignment that would give her greater responsibility and earnings. In the meantime, they made sure that they took a few weekend breaks with each other and at least one fortnight-long vacation every year so they didn't lose touch with each other. It worked for them. But this may not necessarily be the best solution, for in two years, the two partners may have drifted away from each other, or after two years they may be so committed to their work and lifestyles, that they might not want to change things.

5. *Inclusive and exclusive boundaries.* Even though boundaries may be congruent, they may end up excluding the partner. An inclusive boundary is one which takes into consideration the partner's feelings, thoughts or ideas on the matter. The approach then is not just 'your problem and you'd better deal with it'; it becomes 'it may be your problem, but is there anything I can do to help?' Typically, many couples feel that work-related decisions have to be taken in exclusion of the partner, since the latter does not understand one's workplace dynamics or issues. While it is true that you understand your workspace the best, your partner can certainly add some value to your decision-making if you, right from the beginning, make the additional effort of sharing some of the issues in your workplace with your partner, thereby ensuring that your work boundary is not an exclusive one. If you make it exclusive, your partner is completely left out of what is happening in a major chunk of your daily life and this can lead to feelings of disconnectedness.

Rakhi was a homemaker, married to Kaushik,

who worked for his industrialist father's group of companies. Never being particularly interested in business, she found her husband's work-related stories boring. She only kept demanding that he spent more time with her, by itself not an unreasonable expectation. However Kaushik found this hard to do, because he was so preoccupied trying to earn his stripes in the business as well as keeping abreast of all the politics that were taking place at work. He needed to talk about this to somebody sympathetic, but found Rakhi completely unresponsive. As a result, all they ended up doing was fighting, thereby vitiating the home atmosphere. Since she was unwilling to engage with his problems, he refused to engage with what he felt were her petty needs. Therefore they had no platform of communication at all. It's very important for both partners to stay in tune with each other's workspaces (Rakhi's workspace was her home). Considering we spend more than a third of our lives at work, it's absolutely critical that we have a sense of what's happening in our partner's work life. In other words, keep the boundaries inclusive.

6. *Boundary violations.* Even if boundaries are consciously defined, we do tend to violate them every now and again. Sometimes, we violate boundaries intentionally, perhaps out

of anger, maybe out of spite, or even out of sheer contrariness. When such boundary violations happen, a fight invariably ensues. If both partners have agreed that the mobile phone has to be switched off for at least an hour every evening, and one catches the partner furtively sending a work-related text message, a boundary has been violated and there are going to be consequences. If, however, we work out a pattern of dealing with boundary violations, things don't have to necessarily go downhill. It would be useful to remember that not all boundary violations are intentional, but if a repeated pattern of boundary violation persists, then one needs to sit down and review the boundary.

As a general rule, a good way to enhance the quality of a marriage is to ensure that there are as many congruent, relaxed and inclusive boundaries as are humanly possible without, of course, compromising one's quality of working life. And when work demands are a little irrational, spare a thought for your partner, who's waiting for you at home. At least try and get your partner to understand your workspace irrationalities, so there's at least some amount of congruence between the two of you. You might consider doing some of the following to make sure you don't neglect your marriage, even as you attempt to achieve excellence at work.

- Put your mobile phone to good use and stay connected through the day even if it's just a 'Hey, how're you doing?' kind of call. Hearing your partner's voice works better than a text message from your mobile phone's template.

- Try and meet each other during the day, at least a couple of times a week, even if it's just for coffee.

- Wind down together at the end of the day and share what happened to each other at work.

- Switch off your mobile phones for at least an hour or so every evening, so both of you can concentrate on each other.

- Plan at least one 'intimacy evening' a week, so you can recharge your marriage battery regularly. Do whatever pleases both of you on such evenings.

- Try and plan weekend breaks a few times a year. Today, travel websites offer a host of relatively inexpensive opportunities to do so.

- Family budget providing, plan at least one vacation every year, of at least a week's duration, preferably a fortnight.

- During breaks and vacations, try not to spend all your time with your Blackberry, laptop or mobile phone.

- If work-related socialisation is necessary, try and do this together, if it's possible, feasible and acceptable.

- Every now and again, try and socialise as a couple with your respective work colleagues, just so you can put 'faces to the names' that your partner either rants or raves about.

- Have a clear plan as to what kind of goals you have at work, and communicate these to your partner, so both of you are allies in achieving these goals, instead of adversaries coming in each other's way. In general, this will help both of you understand what precisely is to be expected from the work domain.

- Don't permit your workspace to expand so much that it leaves you little room for anything else. Remember, work is only a means to an end, not an end in itself.

THE SOCIAL SPACE—
FRIENDS AND OTHER ENEMIES

Friends and social acquaintances are an important part of life for all of us today. Since the joint family is slowly being denuded, most of us feel the need for a large network of friends as a substitute for the large joint family that most of us in India are accustomed to. In earlier times, most people used to depend on elders in the joint family for advice and guidance, and on cousins, nephews and nieces for recreation and support. Nowadays, friends and acquaintances play these roles in our lives. However, like the large joint family, the social space can also make huge inroads into our personal and marital lives unless we are a little careful.

For as long as he could remember, Maninder had always been a social animal. He had an incredibly large network of social acquaintances and friends. He seemed to be popular with everyone in the city and was always willing to lend a helping hand to anyone in distress. His easy manner, his quick one-liners, his hearty laugh, his readiness to break into a jig, and his large heart drew people to him almost instantly. These were the very reasons that Manpreet, who knew him socially, readily acquiesced when his family sought an alliance with her. She too enjoyed company.

But she also enjoyed her privacy. Maninder had no sense of privacy. He had no clue what to do with himself when alone, and therefore his doors were always open to his friends anytime of the day or night. After they got married, he also became a member of the Round Table and the Rotary. In the first six months of marriage, Manpreet rarely got to spend any time with him alone. Even on their wedding night, at a popular five-star hotel, a large number of his friends dropped into their room for a drink and left only at around 3 in the morning. She was exhausted, but he was all ready to consummate their marriage. Even though they socialised pretty much every day, however late they returned, Maninder charmed her into having sex. Manpreet realised that this was the only time she got to spend alone with her husband, so she stopped complaining. He was rarely rude to her, but she felt like one more member of his large social network, nothing special really. Every time she tried to tell him this, he would fly into a temper, saying she was the only one he had sex with and that's what made their relationship special. However, he always recovered from his anger very soon and was always eager to placate her, although his idea of doing this was to have more sex with her.

Eventually, she tired of their lifestyle and insisted that unless he pull up his socks, she'd return to her parental home. He was bemused. He simply couldn't understand what her problem was, for wasn't he loving to her? Didn't he buy her everything she wanted? Didn't he show her a rocking time? Did he ever neglect her? Did he ever get drunk and beat her? He couldn't for the life of him understand what Manpreet's beef was. His parents suggested that he take her on a holiday, since they'd never been even on a honeymoon. Initially, he made plans to go to Switzerland with four other couples from his Table, but he hastily cancelled them when he saw the expression on her face when she heard of this. Finally, they went to the Maldives and stayed at a luxury resort. The vacation was a disaster, for they realised that they had no clue what to do with each other when they were alone, except to have sex. They returned after three miserable days.

Although Maninder and Manpreet's story may be an extreme one, it is not uncommon to find that many couples permit friends and social acquaintances a lot of space in their lives, even if the marriage suffers in consequence. Taking the *athithi devo bhava* (the guest is God) maxim too seriously can have some lasting consequences on one's marital life. I'm not for a moment suggesting that one shouldn't have friends. I think friends are extremely valuable assets in one's life and the joy they can bring and the support they can provide, are absolutely immeasurable. However, unless we delineate boundaries between our marriage space and friends, the joy and support are slowly going to dwindle and it may not be surprising to find that your friends turn into enemies.

I think by now you understand how to define boundaries between the different spaces in your life, and I am therefore not going to describe the whole process to you again. Use the same principles that you used in defining boundaries between your marriage space, family space and workspace. The key thing is to make sure that you have at least some friendship space so you don't have to lose out on the tremendous benefits that this space can provide you. Pay attention to the following issues that frequently crop up and you'll be able to deal with the boundary definition process effectively.

How much time can we make available to friends? Whom do we socialise more with—my friends, your friends or our friends (the people we click with as a couple)?

How close do we want to get to which of our friends? Just meet them once in a way at parties? Go out on family vacations with them? Help them financially when they're in trouble? Help them emotionally when they're having a bad time? Share our own marital problems with them?

How can we learn to say 'no' to them, if they become too demanding?

How often is a 'night out' with the boys or girls acceptable?

If friends tell us something in confidence, do we keep the confidence or share it with our partner?

Is flirtatious behaviour acceptable? If so, how flirtatious can one get?

If an opposite-gender friend makes a pass, do we just ignore it or talk to our partner about it?

When you think through all of these, and make conscious choices about how both of you, as a couple, as well as individuals, will conduct your respective friendships as well as your joint friendships, and you define boundaries that are congruent, relaxed and inclusive, then friends can, as they are well known to do, add value to your lives.

Before we move on from friendships, there are just two special issues I'd like to consider—using our friends as marriage counsellors and opposite-gender friendships because I've seen both of these sometimes snowball into unmanageable proportions.

Friends as marriage counsellors

It's not uncommon for couples to discuss their marital issues with friends, more likely separately than together. In the past, women tended to do this more frequently than men, more so with their girlfriends. However, in recent times, men too, have started talking about their marital issues with their friends. With the increase in opposite-gender friendships, it is not at all unusual for people to discuss marital issues in the belief that getting an opposite-gender perspective may actually benefit the marriage. Sometimes it does, sometimes things develop differently, as we will examine later. However, the question at hand is how much credibility do our friends have as marriage counsellors? With due respect, I must say, not much.

I don't doubt the good intentions and emotional intensity that friends bring when they counsel you. But when push comes to shove, they are pretty much in the same boat as you are. Whatever solutions have worked for them may or may not work for you, because your realities and experiences are not quite the same as theirs. Your personalities are not identical and therefore, even if you try and implement what they advise, you might find it does not make much difference to your marriage.

Raghu advised his friend Bijoy that the best way to deal with his wife's sexual anxieties was to show her a few pornographic videos. It had worked in his case, and he saw no reason why it shouldn't work in

Bijoy's as well. A sexually desperate Bijoy immediately purchased half a dozen pornographic videos and insisted that he and his wife see them together. She almost threw up in disgust when she saw them. It put her off sex for even longer. What Raghu had not known was that Bijoy's wife had been a victim of sexual abuse during her early adolescence, which was why she was uncomfortable with the idea of sex. Raghu's wife had been merely shy and poorly informed about sex. The videos he had screened for her helped her to relax and educate herself a bit. So it had worked for her. But this was not the appropriate solution for Bijoy's wife.

Additionally, friends do tend to be biased. Your friends will try and persuade you to see the wisdom of your spouse's ways and vice-versa. In this sense, they are not much different from family members. And as we have discussed, once family members enter the marriage, even small issues get unnecessarily escalated and hugely magnified. The same thing often happens when friends intervene. Talking to your friends in a confidential space just to ventilate some of your unhappiness is one thing, but expecting them to provide solutions is another. I find that friendships generally last longer when friends are not expected to intervene *between* the two of you. They're generally better off if they can somehow help *both* of you weather the storm. Here's one more piece of unsolicited advice: if you want to sort out issues in your marriage, see a couples' therapist or a marriage counsellor.

Opposite-gender or platonic friendships

The term 'platonic relationship' refers to any equation between people of different genders that does not include a sexual component, but does include a greater degree of emotional investment than just a casual acquaintanceship. When a man says a woman is his friend, though not his girlfriend, what he's saying is that he cares for her, enjoys her company, is dependent on her for some things in his life and misses her when she is not around, but he cannot think of her as *the* woman in his life for she does not sweep him away, nor is there any sexual tension between them.

However, platonic friendships are not just about asexuality. They are basically relationships that involve an emotional investment. Friends invest feelings in each other, help and support each other, spend time with each other and make a commitment to each other. In the absence of these, a 'friendship', or whatever else you choose to call it, remains a fair-weather equation. Like all other relationships, a friendship also grows. Just like marriage, friendships too have lives of their own and require periodic emotional investment to grow. Which is why we sometimes find ourselves in situations where friendship also tends to add to the demands being made on us.

It is this emotional investment that we need to be cautious about. For, if it comes at the expense of other relationships, the fine balance in our emotional life goes out of kilter. You might find that your partner is not so understanding when it comes to your supporting your platonic friend through some difficult life situation if the energy going your platonic friend's way detracts from or diminishes your marriage. Or you might find your platonic friend gets a bit huffy when you start cancelling your weekly ritual lunches because your work has become very demanding. And you are placed in the unenviable situation of trying to sort out and respond to the various emotional needs your already over-stretched psyche is grappling with. Also, there are situations in life, such as when one is going through an emotional crisis, when even the best of platonic friendships may be severely tested. For, during vulnerable moments, when a woman and a man engage in an intimate conversation, sexual tension is known to have made its unsolicited appearance. How this sexual tension is responded to will determine just how platonic the relationship will remain.

The upshot of what I am saying is this: You have to work as smart on your platonic relationships to keep them platonic as you do at your marriage and other relationships. There's no point in feeling the same way for your platonic friend as you do for your spouse. I remember a husband who complained that his wife did the same things with her platonic friend (except have sex, of course) as she did with him. Naturally, this made him feel insecure and uncomfortable. Intensity can be a two-edged sword, extremely energising on the one hand, but equally depleting on the other. And if you feel as intensely for your platonic friend as you do for your spouse, a crisis is simply waiting to happen. If you find that you're unfavourably comparing your partner's quirks to your friend's calm, or every time you have a work-related problem you run to your friend and not to your partner, or that you can't wait to finish your lunch with your partner so you can meet up with your platonic friend at the neighbourhood coffee shop, then something is happening that even a *rakhi* cannot avert.

However, if you do define your boundaries with your platonic friend and are able to keep your relationship within these, if you keep the intensity down to manageable proportions and do not have irrational expectations, you could well have a long, productive and meaningful friendship, one that does not take away from your other relationships, but enriches you and makes you the better person all of us are trying to become.

14

Fighting Smart

All married couples, even recently married ones, fight. Sometimes we call it a row, sometimes a spat, sometimes a scrap. But whatever it actually is, we do engage in a not always polite exchange of hostilities every now and again. We tell ourselves that it is normal to fight and that everybody is doing it, but there is this sneaking suspicion that maybe we shouldn't be, and that maybe there are better ways to resolve differences of opinion than by hurling juicy epithets, an expensive objet d'art, or breakable ashtrays at each other.

So what's the official word on fights? Most good couples' therapists will tell you that fights are healthy, and if well utilised, even energising for a relationship. I am, of course, not suggesting that you immediately launch into a fight with your partner every time you feel the energies in the relationship are a bit low.

What I am saying is, when two people engage in an honest, close, intimate, communicating relationship where they attempt to share and engage with each other's minds, there is bound to be some friction generated. When couples tell me they don't fight, I'm concerned for their relationship. Not fighting could often, though not always, be a symptom of not engaging with each other. When couples tell me they fight incessantly, I am more concerned with what they fight about than the fact that they fight so much.

The trick with fighting is to fight smart, not hard. In its most basic and simple form, a fight represents a temporary breakdown of love, trust, respect and intimacy between a man and a woman, owing to a gap in communication, understanding or tolerance between the two. Typically, fights happen for a few well-defined reasons.

The Stress-Buster Fight is the most common type of fight and usually happens when one or both partners experience a stressful life experience in a domain outside the marriage—usually at work. A nasty swipe taken at the partner seems to relieve the stress temporarily but when the equally stressed-out partner retaliates, a fight ensues. Pallavi, a TV news channel producer, had a very stressful job. Her hours were not within her control and sometimes, she would be away from home for over 24 hours. Her husband, Arvind, was a doctor earning his post-graduate degree, and he too had to work long hours. Pallavi had a long-standing problem with her boss, but she was reluctant to leave the job because she felt that her boss would soon be sacked. Almost every time she and Arvind met at home, they would fight, invariably over small things. He would take a swipe at her for not organising the dinner, she would snap back at him for not paying the rent on time. There would be a bit of an explosion on both sides for a while, and soon both would recover and get on with their lives.

Stress-buster fights are usually easily resolved provided the swiping partner is a reasonable apologiser, since there are no deeper issues involved. If an apology is not readily forthcoming, such fights too can linger on unnecessarily. The longer they remain unresolved, the more the tension between the partners. What you fought about may be forgotten, but the tension remains—the swiping partner experiences occasional twinges of guilt for being unreasonable and the swiped partner feels righteously indignant.

The Unfulfilled Expectations Fight is very common in the first year of the marriage, for this is the time both partners are in the process of negotiating and clarifying their expectations of each other, figuring out which expectations are irrational and so on.

Mahavir, after several discussions with Lakshmi, had decided that she would never fulfil his expectation of experimenting when they made love. She liked sex only in the missionary position and was unwilling to try even minor variations. He had fantasised about having sex in every room in their house; while they were having a shower, even on the terrace under the stars and in various Kama Sutra positions. She was too straitlaced to indulge all his fantasies, but in all other ways they were perfectly compatible and quite happy with each other. He decided to let go of his fantasies, but often, after they made love, he would snap at her for something inconsequential, and they would end up having a fight about something quite unconnected to his frustration.

The underlying dynamic here is the feeling on the part of one partner that the other is insensitive to her/his needs and expectations, matched by the other's feeling that these expectations are unrealistic. If the couple learns to talk about these issues, the fights need not happen. However, until both partners have learned to moderate their expectations, they may still fight over them. Also, even if one has 'let go' of a particular expectation based on the realisation that it is never going to be fulfilled, there is still a feeling of being short-changed which will last for a while and result in the sort of fight Mahavir and Lakshmi had. It's only when expectations are clarified, marriage templates defined, and the marriage space adequately differentiated (*Chapters 7 & 8*) that these kinds of fights cease.

The Control Fight is something that starts early on in the marriage and can continue throughout its life, unless the couple makes a conscious effort to stop controlling each other by defining personal and marriage spaces. Usually, control fights happen whenever we feel vulnerable or when we feel our identity is threatened, or we feel controlled by our partner's behaviour and feel the need to retaliate. This can also be considered a variation of boundary violation fights (*described below*) for what essentially happens is that one partner, either consciously or inadvertently, violates a boundary and encroaches on the other's personal space.

Rahim was always trying to control the time that Yasmin spent with her sister. He felt that his wife was overly influenced by what he considered her sister's superficial behaviour. He wanted her to be a little more serious in life and get involved in good causes, instead of frittering away her time in shopping, movies and going to coffee shops. Yasmin was very resentful of Rahim's interference in what she believed was her personal space, and both of them would have endless rows on this matter. Since she was a spirited woman, she didn't give in to his demand on her to reduce her contact with her sister. Every time they fought about anything else, they would eventually come back to this unresolved issue. Control fights are very frequent in the early stages of marriage till both partners learn to delineate their respective individual spaces (*Chapters 9 and 10*).

The Umbilical Cord Fight is probably the most intense of all fights because this involves an assessment by one partner that the other is still strongly attached by the emotional umbilical cord to a parent. Until both partners reach a common understanding of the situation and make an attempt to deal with both sets of parents and both umbilical cords together as a joint venture, variations of these fights keep erupting at the most unexpected and awkward of times. Kiran was convinced that her husband, Viren, was a typical Mama's boy. He felt the need to spend inordinate amounts of time with his mother, though he was pretty distant from his father. Every evening, he would report the events of the day to his mother, and would even call her up a couple of times during the day, just to keep in touch with her. Of course, he was attentive to Kiran's needs too, but his cloying dependence on his mother grated on Kiran. Viren simply could not understand why she was being so nasty about his relationship with his mother, when he was so loving to his wife too. Every time Kiran saw mother and son closeted in conversation, she saw red, and a fight would ensue. Soon, she withdrew from him and started spending more time with her parents, much to Viren's bemusement. He too, started taking pot shots at her family.

These kinds of fights will stop only when 'Me and My Family Vs You and Your Family' becomes 'We and our Families' (*Chapter 12*).

The Mixed Signals Fight is easier to resolve although it can be very distressing, because both partners feel victimised by the fight. This fight usually takes place when one partner is signalling for something specific, like say to be parented or fussed over, and the other is completely oblivious to the signals. Most Mars–Venus kind of situations, where partners find it difficult to understand each other's needs because of gender differences, falls in this category.

The Parental Pattern Fight is the most difficult to figure out. Often, we find ourselves repeating our parents' patterns of relating to each other. It's almost like we have a script inherited from our parents and we get affronted when we find that our partner doesn't seem to follow it and, what's worse, seems to be playing out her/his own script which seems absolutely unfathomable. This happens in all marriages, not as a genetic phenomenon but an acquired one. Since our parents' marriage and communication patterns are the first that we've been exposed to, these often form a template around which we model our own relationships.

Catherine's primary marriage template was defined from her grandparents' marriage, since she grew up with them. Her grandmother tended to snap at her grandfather every time the latter bought fish for she was never satisfied with what her husband picked up from the market, even though she refused to go and buy the fish herself. When Catherine got married to

Williams, she insisted that he buy the fish and meat, while she bought the vegetables. He was pretty good at doing this, for he had done it even before they got married. But, whatever he bought, she was never satisfied, and would always complain and bicker about his lack of common sense in such matters. He could never understand her when she did this.

When we become conscious of our primary marriage templates (*Chapter 8*) and learn to define our final marriage templates, this pattern of fight also reduces in frequency and intensity, although occasional residues may creep up, because what we learned as children may sometimes be hard to forget.

The Boundary Violation Fight is the type of fight that stays with us for a long time, largely because, since we are all fallible human beings, we tend to violate even those boundaries that we have consciously agreed to respect. These could be on account of personal space encroachments (*the 'control fight' described earlier*), or violations of boundaries between the marriage space and the other spaces in one's life—family space, work space and friends space. In short, any deviation from agreed-upon behaviour can precipitate a boundary violation fight.

The trick to smart fighting lies in understanding what kind of fight one is having and trying to deal with the root cause. In the final analysis, a fight is a bit like pain. Just as pain is an indicator of some deeper pathology in your body, so too is a fight an indicator of some issue in the marriage. And like pain, fights should never be ignored but always investigated and rooted out, not with a pain-killer, but by treating the cause. Without pain would we know pleasure? Without fights would we know marital bliss?

RULES FOR FIGHTING SMART

To get the best out of your fights, which is what smart fighting is all about, you could try to utilise the following ground rules that many couples have benefited from.

> *Rule #1. It takes two to fight, so don't wait for your partner to initiate the making up.* The initial making up serves to reduce the tensions between both of you, and even though the fight may not yet be resolved, this stage needs to be gone through. For only when the anger and hostility has disappeared can both of you start talking about the fight. You apologise for *your role* in the fight. Whoever started the fight, if the other had not responded with aggression, the fight would never have happened, would it? So, taking responsibility for your role in the fight is not tantamount to saying that you caused it.

> *Rule #2. Make up only when you're good and ready to do so.* Many couples believe in the aphorism '*Never*

go to sleep on a fight'. As a result, come what may, before they go to sleep, they feel compelled to make up. *Compulsive making-up* can result in long-term resentment and a feeling that one has compromised one's needs just to obtain peace at any cost. In this situation, the one who initiates the making-up ends up subtly taking the responsibility for the fight. So make up only when a fair proportion of your anger has dissipated and you feel ready to do so. However, don't dawdle over making up. Get good and ready soon. Never more than 24 hours at the maximum.

Rule #3. When both of you have cooled off, analyse the fight. Do this as a discipline. Of course, I don't mean a lengthy and detailed analysis or a fault-finding analysis. The object of analysing the fight is to genuinely understand WHAT caused it, not WHO caused it. Typically, at the end of an analysis, both of you would have realised what kind of fight took place and why.

Rule #4. Don't waste your time on the sequence of events that led to the fight when you analyse it. You'll find that in most of your fights, you spend only about 90 seconds fighting about whatever provoked either of you. The rest of the time you are either fighting about the way you fight or saying mean things to each other designed to hurt or bringing up residues of past fights. This is true regardless of what you're fighting about and what type of a fight took place.

Rule #5. What's said in anger, is not necessarily what one truly feels. There is a popular belief that, if one says something when one's drunk or angry, what is said is invariably the truth. Not true at all. When one is drunk, one's mind is completely confused and one says nonsensical things. When one is angry, one ends up saying mean and nasty things because one wants to hurt the partner. One can certainly regret saying mean and nasty things, and often people do, but when the partner refuses to accept the apology because of this belief, things can run adrift.

Rule #6. If it's a stress-buster fight, let things go. No sense in over-analysing this one. But try not to dismiss all your fights as belonging to this category. Many couples do, for this is the easiest way of dealing with a fight. And since most of us are under some stress or other most of the time, it's very tempting to attribute all fights to stress. Typically, in a stress-buster fight, you will experience relief and feel light once the fight is over. It is like someone lanced an abscess, releasing all toxic waste from inside your mind. Therefore, your good humour is restored very soon and you find it easy to apologise. If, at the end of your fight, you're still angry and feeling depleted instead of relieved, then it's not a stress-buster fight.

Rule #7. Figure out what type of fight took place, if it was not a stress-buster fight. Use the guidelines in the previous section to do this. You might well find that some of your fights don't fall in the above categories. In this case create your own categories. But wherever you peg it, try and understand which emotions led both of you to fight.

Rule #8. Don't be judgemental when you analyse the fight. Also, don't feel defensive or superior. Remember, the object of analysis is not to play the *blame game*. Just try and understand what happened, so both of you can try not to repeat the pattern.

Rule #9. Keep an open mind. Even if you don't come to an immediate conclusion on how to resolve the issue at hand, it doesn't matter. Keep the dialogue going so you can re-address and resolve it at a later date.

Rule #10. Employ mutually comfortable making-up strategies. 'Make-up sex' is a much hyped method of dealing with the negative fallouts of a fight. However, most couples don't necessarily find it the best way to make up. Whatever comes naturally to both of you is the best way. Whether you're going to do the flowers-and-card routine, or just hold each other, or go out somewhere special, or anything else you can think of, is entirely your own business.

Fights can actually do the marriage some good, if we approach them sensibly. They are usually cues that something is happening under the surface, and if we devote some time and energy to understanding these, we can actually get closer to our partner. There's no point in being upset that you fight. If you learn to fight smart, you'll find that whatever energies you have dissipated in the fight will be a small price to pay for getting to know your partner better. However, just make sure that you fight smart, and not hard.

15

Smart Communication Basics

One way to make sure that fights are completely resolved is to ensure that one gets the communication basics right. This is required not just for conflict resolution, but also to enhance intimacy. Often, communication ends up getting reduced to grunts, monosyllables and i luv u txt msgs. Can't we do better than this? If you would like to, keep some of these communication basics in mind.

Communication requires time

So, over a hurried breakfast is never the best time to talk about anything other than asking, 'Some more coffee?' Also required is a relaxed atmosphere where a couple can talk to each other without too many interferences. I know that we live in an age of multi-tasking, but your partner's not going to buy your argument that you can watch television and engage in meaningful conversation at the same time. So, set aside the remote control, close the laptop, shut off your mobile phone (or at least switch it on silent and keep it out of view, so you don't keep glancing at it furtively every time it glows), and concentrate on communication mono-tasking.

Listen to what your partner is saying

This may seem a completely unnecessary thing to say, but you'd be surprised at how little we listen to what our partner is saying. As a rule of thumb, men are pretty poor listeners, but in recent times, I find that women are giving them quite a run for their money in the deaf adder department. Since we live in such a fast-paced world, we want everything to happen like a Twenty20 cricket match, and are generally too impatient to listen to what our partner is saying. When I say 'listen to your partner', I don't mean 'keep quiet while your partner is talking'. I mean try and engage with what is being said. Typically, when our partner is saying something, we hear only the first sentence or so and are busy with whatever emotions that first sentence evokes in us and marshal our thoughts on what to say in reply. If both of you catch yourselves doing this, remember that your communications to each other are not being adequately received.

What you might consider using is the *'my airtime, your airtime'* strategy. Each gives the other five uninterrupted minutes to say what they want on the subject. During this time, the speaker speaks, and the listener listens. No interruptions. No clarifications. Only after the speaker has finished may the other respond to what has been said. Each partner gets their airtime alternately. However, let this not turn into a lecture or monologue. Five minutes of talking should be good enough. Try not to use a stopwatch, though.

Talk TO each other, not AT each other

Couples, particularly those who don't listen to each other, end up talking AT each other. By this I mean that the other person is expected to be merely a passive recipient. It could be anybody at the other end, even the dog. One is not really engaging with the other person or what is being said; one has something to say and will say it in as many ways as possible, without even attempting to take in what the other person is saying or doing. Eye contact is minimal. You end up sounding like you're giving *gyan*, or a lecture, or a monologue. Even if, by virtue of some inherent politeness, you allow your partner to talk, you're not really listening or engaging with what is being said. However, when you talk TO each other, it's not so much about just getting your message across, it's equally about receiving your partner's message, even if you completely disagree with what your partner's trying to say. The important thing is that it is sinking in, and your response to what has been said will, therefore, be appropriate and considered.

Talk through the issue, not around it

Probably, one reason why so many communication gaps exist between couples is on account of the tendency to talk around an issue. When one talks through an issue, one deals with the issue completely. One confronts it head on and one tries to express one's position on the matter as simply and clearly as possible. However, it is not often that we have a stomach for head-on confrontation, since we fear that it could turn messy. So we talk around it; we hedge a bit and try to 'give hints' to our partner rather than saying things directly. We end up thinking we've communicated what we wanted to say, but actually the partner has understood it completely differently. Talking around the issue can actually involve a lot a peripheral talk without getting to the issue at hand.

For instance, a woman wants to tell her husband why her mother-in-law bothers her so much. So she starts off at a tangent, by explaining to him how difficult her work is and how much pressure she is under and how, when she comes back home and finds her mother-in-law looking so unhappy, it brings her down even more, and so on. She's actually very angry with her mother-in-law for making snide comments about women going to work and leaving older people at home to do all the work. But she hasn't come to this yet. Her husband's interpretation of whatever she's saying is completely different. He thinks she's trying to ventilate to him about how stressful her work is and suggests that she should try and look for another job, and is also touched that she feels so much about his mother's unhappiness, and wonders whether including his mother in their forthcoming holiday plans would help. This is one example of talking around an issue. There are many other variations, but the basic problem is that the issue is not addressed in depth, and at the end of the transaction, there is a feeling of incompleteness in the mind of at least one, if not both, partners.

Communication is not always about solutions

Living as we do in an age of solution-providers, it is our instinctive tendency to try and quickly find a solution to a spouse's problem. In the past, this kind of response used to be the man's prerogative, but not any more. Women too deal with many situations the same way. The net result is that one of the principal objects of communication—the opportunity to be heard—gets completely negated. Within the first few minutes of your partner's communication, you have already come to a diagnostic conclusion, worked out a solution and have, in effect, stopped listening any more. If you are polite, you might wait for your partner to finish, or if you're in a hurry, you might jump in with a solution and end up causing frustration, because what was expected of you was not the solution (maybe your partner has already figured out the solution). Try responding to your partner's cues in this situation. If, for instance, your partner starts off by saying, 'Look, I'm having this problem and want to bounce something off you', well then obviously an approach to a solution has already been figured out and your partner wants to share what's happening in her/his mind. If, on the other hand, your partner says, 'I'm completely stuck with this problem. What do you think I should do?', this would perhaps be a good time to come in with a solution.

Men and women communicate differently

It has now been well established that men and women think differently, respond differently in the same situation and communicate differently. I am not going into detail about these differences in communication patterns between the genders, since several books have been written on the subject. (If you're interested, you can read *Men are from Mars, Women are from Venus* by John Gray and *Why Men Don't Listen and Women Can't Read Maps* by Allan and Barbara Pease). But the point I'm trying to make is that men and women are different. If you find you're not able to completely understand what your partner is saying despite your best attempts to do so, or if your partner receives your communication quite differently, despite your best attempts at clarity, I'd say you've hit the 'gender wall'. In this case, you need to make more effort to understand each other. Both the books I've mentioned will help to this end.

Communication is not always about agreement

It's not necessary that, at the end of a good communication, both of you see things the same way. If this happens, it's a nice little bonus. But don't start communicating with the belief that you need to convince your partner of your position. As long as your partner is able to see what your position is, even if there is no agreement on the issue, you've done your job.

The use of 'I' and 'You' words

When one wants to get a message across to one's partner, using the 'You' word is best avoided. When one starts off a sentence with 'You', the partner always perceives it as an accusatory statement, whether it's meant that way or not. Whereas when you start off with 'I', the implication is that it is a clarificatory statement. For example, when you say 'You didn't call me the whole of today', you're making an accusation against your partner, which may result in unnecessary defensiveness and a tangential response like, 'When will you ever be satisfied with me?' Whereas, if you put it differently, using the 'I' word, say 'I get worried when you don't call', your partner feels less accused and will more likely respond to you in a conciliatory manner than an aggressive one.

'Never' and 'Always'

These are two words that should be completely removed from a couple's communication lexicon. Typical examples.

'*You* never *come home on time.* ' ('*Of course not. I came home early last Saturday.*')

'*You're* always *being nasty to my mother.*' ('*Don't be silly. I'm never nasty to her.*')

While you may be using these two words to emphasise your point, they end up diverting the conversation and the rest of the communication centres around trying to prove the inaccuracy of your statement. Also, it signifies a greater accusatory tone than is necessary for healthy communication.

16

Some Special Situations

In the preceding chapters, I have attempted to explore the issues that are generic to most New Indian Marriages. But I am aware that there are situations that may be specific only to some, not all marriages. Obviously, one cannot cover all specific issues in a book of this sort, but there are some issues that crop up more often than they should, so I'd like to spend a little time on each of these. These are issues that may require to be handled with some measure of delicacy, tact and understanding. Hopefully, a brief overview might help—if at least to nudge you in the right direction.

PRE-MARITAL NON-DISCLOSURES

Neena, a graphic designer by training but a homemaker by choice, was told that the bridegroom identified for her in Australia was a chartered accountant working in a large international bank. Several months after living in Australia with him, in a chance conversation with her neighbour, she came to know that Ashutosh, her husband, had actually never been to college, and worked in this large international bank as a teller.

Maqbool and Zahira were reasonably happy after two years of marriage, when he found a job in Muscat. When he took her passport to apply for a visa, he realised that she was eleven months older than he was. Both were aghast. He, because this was not what her father had told him at the time of the alliance. She, because she thought he was aware of it and was liberal enough in his thinking not to mind.

Joseph and Jessica met on an Internet matrimonial site and got married after both their respective families had established comfort levels with each other. Six months after the wedding, when they were investigating his erectile dysfunction, she learned from his doctor that Joseph's anti-epileptic medication could be the cause of the problem, but under no circumstances was he to stop the medication, for he had his last fit as recently as eight months ago. Needless to say, this came as a shock to Jessica, for this was the first time she was hearing of his epilepsy.

Even in New Indian Marriages, some amount of pre-marital non-disclosure does take place. Some facts are actively suppressed, some not made explicit ('but you never asked!') and some just hinted at, before the wedding takes place. How the 'deceived partner' reacts when matters come out into the open, as they inevitably will (how long can you keep your job, your age or a major illness under wraps?), cannot really be predicted. From my experience, I'd hazard to say, even though I don't have hard data, that more than a third of marriages where this form of non-disclosure took place, ended up in the Family Court.

Every time I speak to the non-disclosing family and ask them why they did what they did, they are invariably filled with remorse. They tell me that the primary reason for non-disclosure was the fear that the truth might mean the loss of a perfectly good alliance. What they never contemplated was that the truth would come out at some time or the other, and when it did, however long the couple had been married, however strong the bond they had developed during this period, the 'non-disclosing' partner would come under severe pressure, and experience indescribable humiliation. Even if such a partner were not aware of, nor party to, the non-disclosure (e.g. Zahira's story described earlier), they are not believed by their partners. The essential trust in the partner and the marriage is lost and if the 'deceived' partner does decide to stay in the marriage, a long and painful process of re-building trust has to be undertaken. Also, the balance of power in the marriage tilts and the 'non-disclosing' partner is expected to shoulder the primary burden of this re-building process.

Frankly, the best way to deal with this is prevention. Make sure that nothing is kept away from the partner. There's no need to overdo it either. Your partner does not need to know that you had chicken pox when you were nine and measles when you were six. However, if you had mumps in childhood, as a result of which you've become sterile, you should tell your prospective partner about it. Anything major that will have some form of impact on your partner's perception of or comfort with you, is better shared.

This may bring you face to face with certain dilemmas. If for example, a woman's fiancé is a sexually experienced man but insists that his bride be a virgin, and the woman has told him that she is one, despite having had multiple sexual partners and two abortions earlier, then believe me, she is asking for trouble. In this situation, the woman may feel she can fool him into thinking she's a virgin, and some women may actually be able to pull it off, but it's an extraordinary risk where the chance of discovery is high. My recommendation is to be open before you get married.

A word to the 'deceived partner': Try not to be too harsh when you come across a non-disclosure of this sort. I do agree that it can rock your trust in your partner, but try and understand that it took place in a certain context. Because you were considered a good alliance, your partner's family probably did some window-dressing, which they, in hindsight, perhaps should not have done. If you find that in other ways, your partner is reasonably good for you, try and practise some forgiveness. It might actually make for a long and stable marriage.

PAST RELATIONSHIPS

Most people in contemporary urban life have at least one ex before they get married, even if theirs is an arranged marriage. So getting worked up about your partner's ex or exes is rather futile. The question is whether or not you share your past romantic history with your partner.

Smita was uncomfortable about her husband Anirudh's best friend from his school days—Priti, who was apparently quite happily married to Harbhajan. Smita didn't particularly mind Anirudh having a woman as a best friend, but the intimacy that the two of them seemed to share raised her hackles. She asked him whether they'd ever been romantically involved. He denied it vehemently, and so she stopped asking him about it. But she continued to have some misgivings. Everybody in their social circle (mainly his friends, since she was from another city) sniggered when they saw her looking worriedly at Anirudh and Priti sharing a joke or teaming up successfully in a game of Pictionary or dancing the salsa together.

Harbhajan seemed blasé about the whole thing. This reassured her a bit. It also helped that Anirudh was actually a good husband to her. He seemed to like her, and both of them had some really great times. The sex was terrific and she did not have any in-law problems. Except for the Anirudh-Priti connection, everything was fine. Once, at a party, a friend spilled the beans. Seeing Smita's discomfiture with Priti's and Anirudh's horsing around, one of their friends loudly remarked to her, 'Don't worry, Smita. Their relationship was over long before you came on the scene.' Everyone laughed, including Harbhajan, who apparently knew that Anirudh was his wife's ex.

Everyone, except Smita and Anirudh. Smita looked terribly upset and on the verge of crying. Anirudh looked irritated, but also embarrassed. Priti's laughter got stuck in her throat when she saw Anirudh's expression. 'You, mean, you haven't told her about our past?' she asked Anirudh, who silently looked away. Everyone felt silent. Harbhajan tried to reassure Smita, telling her that his wife and her husband were only friends now, though they did have a history. They were in a relationship but felt that they had to terminate it because their friendship was suffering and they were not really suited to each other. The party broke up soon after. Priti started cooling off towards Anirudh for she could not understand why he hadn't told Smita. Anirudh tried to tell Smita that he didn't want her to feel insecure, which was why he had never said anything about his relationship with Priti. Smita was absolutely humiliated, not because he'd had a relationship with Priti, but because she was the only person in the 'gang' who didn't know about it even though she was his wife and supposedly the most important person in his life. Soon the 'gang' drifted apart and stopped seeing each other.

Here, too, non-disclosure about the past led to substantial problems in the marriage. As a rule of thumb, complete disclosure is always safer. However, if your peccadilloes happened in the dim and distant past, then complete disclosure may lead to unnecessary problems. Kamini came from a lower-middle-class background from a small town. While in college she had a romantic liaison with a classmate to whom she wanted to get married. However, both families were against the match and used considerable pressure to quash the relationship. Subsequently, she concentrated on her career and almost eight years later entered into an arranged marriage with Sushil, who was a simple and straightforward sort of person. On their wedding night, Kamini felt obliged to tell Sushil about her old and long-forgotten affair. He was devastated, for he had always dreamed of marrying a 'pure' woman. He just couldn't touch her because he felt she had been defiled. She was filled with guilt for tormenting a good man with her 'shady' past. It took them more than a year to get past this revelation.

If indeed you are going to disclose past

relationships, the wedding night or any day after the wedding is not a good idea. Do so before the wedding, or if you feel the past relationship is not critical to your current life or your future, simply don't worry about it. However, if your partner asks you a leading question, don't duck it. A lie is far more difficult to survive than passive non-disclosure.

JUST POSSESSIVE OR IS THERE AN OTHELLO AT HOME?

In the early throes of love, many couples pass through a phase where they are 'possessive' of each other and 'jealous' of anyone else who is in any way emotionally close to the partner. In fact, it is sometimes said that you can't be in love if you don't feel possessive about your partner. A young man came to see me once, questioning the depth of his girlfriend's love for him, for she never became jealous of any other woman he was friendly with, however hard he tried to make her react with jealousy. Even in arranged marriages, the more romantically inclined the partners, the more possessive and jealous they tend to get. Although possessiveness is probably better than detachment or indifference, uncontrolled, it can have disastrous consequences. The newspapers and news channels are full of horror stories of the gory things jealous and possessive partners do to each other and to themselves. While these are, of course, extreme scenarios and certainly not the run-of-the-mill end result of possessive behaviour, one needs to realise that possessiveness and jealousy are potentially destructive phenomena, that need to be recognised as problem behaviours and corrected, since they could result in suspecting a partner's fidelity, pathological jealousy— or the Othello syndrome.

Swapna hated it when Nitin spent any part of his free time doing anything that involved being away from her. In fact, she wished she could be working in the same office with him so she could be around him all the time. Not that she did not trust him. She was sure that Nitin would not do anything to hurt or upset her, but she was not sure about the women he interacted with. She was resentful of the fact that he spent more time with his work colleagues than he did with her. She was also very protective of him, especially when any member of his family said or did anything to upset him. She wished she could take him away from his family and look after him. She wanted him on an island, where he could be only hers and nobody else's. This is possessiveness. When one is possessive of one's partner, one feels the need to maintain a certain degree of exclusiveness in the relationship and does not want to share the loved object with anyone else. One would expect that after a period of time, once their relationship stabilises, Swapna will get more relaxed and stop being so possessive and protective of Nitin.

Like Swapna, Indranil too started off by being a little possessive of Mithali and jealous of any man that she interacted with. When one of her male colleagues dropped her home from work on his motorcycle, he was upset about this for days on end. Mithali was actually pleased when he was jealous of her male friends, for it made her feel that he loved her very much. She too was a little jealous of his female friends, but perhaps, not as much as he was. She started getting a little uncomfortable when he started checking her mobile phone to see her message and call logs. She protested, but he reassured her that any man in love with his wife would do this, and that it was only a reflection of how much he loved her. Since he was the one who set her e-mail accounts, he knew her passwords, and once when she came into the room where the home computer was, she saw that he was scrolling through her e-mails. He quickly shut off the computer and told her she was imagining things.

Once, she ran into an old, very good male friend of hers at a coffee shop and he appeared to be awkward and cagey with her. When she asked him what the matter was, he told her he was still offended by her last e-mail to him in which she had told him that she did not want to maintain any contact with him because she loved only her husband and felt uncomfortable about writing to any other man. In the mail, she had also questioned his decency in maintaining a relationship with a married woman.

Mithali was shocked to hear this, for she had never sent such a mail. Suddenly, it started making sense to her why all her old male friends had stopped writing to her or taking her calls. She confronted Indranil, who denied having sent any e-mails in her name. She was positive that he was responsible even though she had no evidence. She changed her password and took charge of her e-mail account. This upset him no end. Soon he started accusing her of writing to her boyfriends on the sly, and took to repeatedly cross-questioning her so he could 'trip her up in a lie'.

She spoke to her family and his. Her family asked her to leave him at once, for they'd never really liked him and had relented only because she'd insisted on marrying him. His family brushed it aside saying he was just a little insecure and advised her on how to make him feel more secure, which involved her changing her whole lifestyle completely and centring her life around his. Things became worse when she overheard a telephone conversation from which it became apparent that he was trying to find a detective agency that would keep an eye on her. She walked out.

Indranil's possessiveness crossed the line of rationality when he started doubting Mithali's fidelity. This form of suspicious behaviour is often seen as a sign of insecurity, which means that one is so afraid of losing the loved object that one needs to hunt for potential threats in the environment. It usually springs from low self-esteem, which makes the individual feel unworthy of the partner. However, with growing comfort in the relationship, such insecurities generally tend to get banished, and couples enter a phase of mutual acceptance and comfort. Sometimes, this is not the case and the possessiveness, jealousy and suspiciousness become progressively worse and enter the realm of irrationality. At this time it becomes a mental health problem, no longer correctable by mere reassurance and 'good behaviour'. It's referred to as the *Othello syndrome* or *morbid jealousy* or *delusional disorder*. Whatever it's called, psychiatric assistance is called for. If it's allowed to progress, it just becomes worse and could end up having the kind of gory consequences that news channels and newspapers report ('*Man Kills Wife and Self*').

The long and short of it is that if your partner is possessive or jealous, don't encourage it. Try reassurance, but don't make major changes in your lifestyle that make you uncomfortable, just to accommodate your partner's irrational needs. Stop any flirtatious behaviour if this is part of your repertoire, reduce your non-critical one-on-one contact with the opposite gender, but don't terminate all your relationships just to cater to your partner. If despite reassurance, the jealousy proceeds to doubting your fidelity and you know perfectly well that you've given no basis for these doubts, it is time to seek the assistance of a psychiatrist. As with all psychiatric problems, the earlier you seek help, the easier the cure. In the final analysis, I know the fair Desdemona was considered a queen among women, a woman of uncommon beauty and chastity, but look what happened to her!

Although it's called the Othello syndrome, it can affect both women and men. So your wife could turn out to be an Othello as well. Being loved 'not wisely, but too well' is not a fate that you would like to be a victim of.

VIOLENCE AT HOME—EVEN ONCE IS TOO MUCH

Domestic violence, as it is officially called, has been happening for centuries in our country and is very much part of 'Indian culture'. It has caused immeasurable grief, much damage to dignity and self-esteem and even incalculable loss of life and limb. Yet it continues to exist and has now reached almost epidemic proportions, thereby shaking even the government of India out of its customary stupor to enact a law to respond to the phenomenon. Though it is debatable whether legislation is the final solution to the problem, in the absence of anything else, I hope the law serves at least to highlight the growing menace of domestic violence. I am well aware that the Domestic Violence Act is abused as much as it's appropriately used and that some women with axes to grind against their husbands, use the Act as a threat to coerce their husbands into doing what they want them to. Despite this, people have begun to generally think a bit before harassing the wife or daughter-in-law.

When I talk of domestic violence, I am referring only to the type of violent behaviour and abuse that takes place between married partners, although social scientists use the term to refer to a larger range of violent acts at home. There are three ways in which spouses abuse each other. The first of these is the most basal of them all—*physical abuse*, where one partner slaps, hits, kicks or beats up the other. Also basal is *sexual abuse*, where the dominant partner engages in marital rape, or forces the partner to have sex even when the latter doesn't want to, or engages in sexually perverse acts without the explicit consent of the partner. Then there is *verbal abuse*, where the abuser regularly resorts to shouting at the partner, using foul and vulgar language. And finally, there is *emotional abuse* wherein one partner subjugates the other through persistent demeaning, insults, threats, and intellectual battering.

Many people think that abuse happens only in lower socio-economic backgrounds. Nothing could be further from the truth. Middle-class homes see large amounts of domestic violence, as do wealthier ones. Also, there is a fallacious belief that a potential abuser can be easily identified. Don't fool yourself. A potential abuser can appear to be a very mild-mannered person. The only thing that one can say with any degree of certainty is that the children of spouse abusers are more likely to abuse their spouses. Also, though technically the abuser could belong to either gender, and there is enough evidence to conclude that, even in our country, women too abuse men, it is far more common to see male abusers than female abusers. Alcoholism and spouse abuse usually share a close relationship, thereby providing the abusive spouse with what is considered an excellent alibi ('it was the alcohol, not I'). And in recent times, life and work-related stress has also become a very common 'justification' for knocking the spouse around.

Typically, as described by social scientists, what one sees in the abusive relationship is a repetitive cyclical pattern. Slowly, over a variable period of time, a tension starts building up in the relationship. The abuser's level of irritability progressively increases and the recipient of the abuse starts engaging in a variety of distracting and avoiding behaviours. This further angers the abuser, who uses this as an excuse (along with alcohol, among other things) to commit the abusive act. This is followed by extraordinary remorse, self-debasing apologies and elaborate making-up rituals that culminate in a honeymoon period of great love, closeness and intimacy, which makes the battered spouse feel is worth the pain of the abuse. However, over a period of time, the honeymoon period starts dwindling in both intensity and duration, but by this time, the abused spouse is pretty much locked into this 'death dance', from which she finds it extremely difficult to break free. In other words, both partners end up perpetuating the pattern, one actively and the other passively.

The mindset of the abuser can be pretty complicated and the reasons for choosing an abusive style of functioning are often pretty complex. The need to control and intimidate is foremost on the mind of the abuser, who does feel remorse for his actions, at least initially, although later this is replaced by indifference.

The way I see it, there is only one way to deal with the situation if your partner gets abusive—physically, verbally, sexually or emotionally. Don't accept it. Approach it with a zero-tolerance policy, so both of you can seek professional help early to resolve the problem. And in this case, the right professional to see would be a mental health professional (psychiatrist, psychologist or trained counsellor). And the sooner you do so, the better it will be, since, once the abusive pattern gets established, it becomes very resilient and very difficult to break. So, if both of you are agreed that even once is too much, you can take reparative action, if the need arises. I'm hoping it doesn't.

ADULT SURVIVORS OF CHILD SEXUAL ABUSE

In our country, we engage in a remarkable defence mechanism called denial, whereby we simply deny to ourselves the existence of some social evils. One such is child sexual abuse, which we have started talking about only in the last few years, and that too only because of concerted efforts on the part of writers, activists, mental health professionals and non-governmental organisations who have espoused the cause and bellowed about it from whichever rooftop they could find.

This has led many people to think of child sexual abuse as a recent phenomenon. More denial. Let me assure you that child sexual abuse has been around in our country for many, many years. And if you still don't believe it's as much of a serious problem as I am making it out to be, kindly get yourself a copy of the Ministry of Women and Child Development of the Government of India's report of the 'National Study on Child Abuse: India 2007', that dropped a bombshell by noting that '53.22 per cent of children all over the country reported having faced one or more forms of sexual abuse' (*when I last checked, it was available online at http://wcd.nic.in/childabuse.pdf*). Over one half of our children are victims of sexual abuse and we are still either ambivalent or in denial about it. I am not going to get into the phenomenon of child sexual abuse in detail, for it is beyond the scope of this book. If you are interested I would recommend you get hold of and read a copy of Pinki Virani's *Bitter Chocolate*, an eye-opener of a book. What I would like to look at is the impact of child sexual abuse on marriage.

People who have been sexually abused as children do survive into adulthood, and do end up getting married. Since the abuse was so traumatic and since it took place when they were very young children, it is buried in the corner of their minds. If ever you find that your spouse is a survivor of child sexual abuse, please don't take him or her to task for not telling you about it before the wedding. Don't treat it as premarital non-disclosure, for this is not the case at all. As I said, the events are often buried in the recesses of the mind, and memories get re-activated only when the victims engage in an intimate relationship of their own. In some situations, for instance if the abuse happened when they were slightly older children, the survivor may recall the event well and may even share it with you during the courtship or engagement period. If they do share it, try and remember that it is perhaps one of the most difficult things in life for them to share, and they are really doing you an honour by sharing it with you.

Try not to react the way Nagesh did when his fiancée, Anusuya, told him of her experience. When she was ten, a year or so before she had her first menstrual period, Anusuya's maternal uncle came to stay with them. He was estranged from his wife and Anusuya's father had offered that he stay with them while he worked through his marital issues. Anusuya was always fond of this uncle, for he would joke and play with her and devise all sorts of games that gave her a lot of pleasure. However, this time around, he devised a game that was a little more sinister. Every time he found where she had hidden a soft toy, she had to kiss any part of his body he chose. Every time he didn't, he would kiss any part of her body she chose. Thus, he made her a partner in the game and, over the weeks, he had kissed her all over her body including on her genitals, which he seemed to enjoy the most. Every time he won, he would make her stroke and kiss his genitals. The fact that all this was done furtively made her suspect that what they were doing was somehow wrong. Also, the fact that her uncle had warned her not tell anybody else about their game and threatened her with dire consequences ('All your hair will fall off, if you tell anybody'; 'I'll never talk to you again', and so on) if she did, made her feel uncomfortable about playing it. However, it seemed to give him so much joy, and he was so affectionate to her through this whole period, that she set her discomfiture aside and went along.

It was only when, one day when her parents had to go out of town, he tried to penetrate her, that she was alarmed. Since it hurt her too much, he tried to get her to perform oral sex. She nearly choked and ran away from the room in tears. He knew he had gone too far. He threatened her never to tell anyone about this, or he would physically harm her. She was terrified and held her tongue. Her mother found it strange that she didn't seem to like her favourite uncle any more, but since he left their home soon after, nobody thought much about it. Except she. She grew into a nervous and anxious teenager and couldn't get close to boys even though all her friends had boyfriends. She couldn't bear to be touched by anybody, leave alone hugged. Slowly, the pain eased and by the time she finished college, she'd forgotten about it. It was only when her wedding was fixed and her aunts were ragging her, saying she couldn't remain an 'ice queen' anymore, that she remembered what had happened to her.

Since her fiancé, Nagesh, seemed like a nice and understanding young man, she decided that she would tell him about what happened to her when she was a child. She had never in her wildest dreams anticipated that he would react the way he did. He accused her of complicity in the relationship with her uncle even though she'd only been ten at the time, felt that she was stained and 'second-hand', told his parents about it as well as hers, and insisted on calling off the engagement. Her parents were shocked and couldn't believe her story for she had told them nothing all those years ago. Her maternal uncle denied that such a thing ever happened and suggested that perhaps she had come up with such a story to get out of marrying Nagesh. She was the villain of the family for nothing that was of her doing. Sadly, she decided she couldn't live down the ignominy of what had happened and committed suicide.

Happily, not all survivors of child sexual abuse suffer Anusuya's fate. But they have an extremely difficult time. Not only do they have to deal with the trauma of the abuse, they also have to deal with the sometimes insensitive responses of people around them, for when they need understanding and empathy, they are not always fortunate to receive it. If you find that your partner is an adult survivor of child sexual abuse, please be sensitive and understanding. With your love and support such victims can overcome their trauma and lead perfectly normal lives. Seeing a mental health professional may help in speeding up the recovery process.

It is also worth noting that, although less commonly than girls, young boys are also victims of sexual abuse. Their abusers are usually older males in their environment—family members, friends, older boys, and so on. However, in some situations, they can also be sexually abused by older, sexually frustrated women.

Sometimes you may never know that your partner was sexually abused as a child unless some manifestations are present. Typically, adult survivors of child sexual abuse tend to have severe issues around their sexual functioning, in that they may find it distasteful to engage in sex. Sometimes, the opposite may happen and they may display sexually promiscuous forms of behaviour in adulthood. Even if this is the case, they may find it extremely difficult to experience and express intimacy in their personal relationships.

The other big issue in the minds of adult survivors of child sexual abuse is trust. Invariably, their abuser in childhood is an older person they instinctively trusted and perhaps even looked up to. So when their trust has been betrayed, they find it difficult to trust in their adult relationships.

Whatever the individual variation, adult survivors of child sexual abuse need to be handled with compassion and dignity. Remember that one out every two of us has been a victim to unwanted sexual attentions from a loved, trusted and respected adult, when we were young and had no idea what sex was. Try and imagine how traumatising it must have been. Help your partner through this by reading about the subject and talking to a mental health professional. I have known many people who have nurtured their abused partners and helped them recover trust and the capacity for intimacy completely, and have, in the process, made very happy marriages for themselves. It is possible, if you set your mind to it.

LETTING THE LAW INTO YOUR MARRIAGE

Letting the law into your marriage is tantamount to sounding its death knell. The newspapers are full of stories of couples and families who take their marriage issues to police stations, panchayats, civil courts and other systems set up to dispense justice. Often, what is reported are the few success stories. How the police united a couple who were squabbling, how conjugal rights were restituted by a court of law, and so forth. However, take it from me, the minute you permit the civil or criminal justice system to enter your marriage, you have ensured that the bond remains a legal one, not an emotional one. Your partner may stay in the marriage and perform the duties of a spouse, but is unlikely to forgive you for having filed a police complaint that resulted in deep humiliation at the time.

Within six months of marriage, Radha was disillusioned by her uncommunicative husband, Pravin, who made no attempt to consummate the marriage. He, coming from a lower socio-economic background, was quite intimidated by her wealth and awed by her father's social status. However, instead of taking professional help, which would probably have been the wisest thing to do, her aggressive and domineering father, a lawyer, who had paid a handsome dowry to get his daughter married, decided to teach the young man a lesson he would never forget. Accordingly, they filed a case against him and his family in the nearby police station under Section 498-A of the Indian Penal Code (this was before the Domestic Violence Act was enacted), which protects women from being subject to cruelty by their husbands and in-laws.

The police was initially reluctant to file the FIR (First Information Report) for they knew this would not be in the couple's best interests, and tried to counsel both partners. Radha's father insisted on the FIR being registered and even obtained a court order to do so. The police had no option but to arrest Pravin and his parents, who were the co-accused. Pravin's family, enraged by the filing of the case, engaged the most prominent lawyer in town, and filed a suit against the girl for restitution of conjugal rights, alleging that the non-consummation of the marriage was owing to her non-compliance. In the course of two acrimonious years, all sorts of legal battles were fought, until finally, at the initiative of a community elder, everybody agreed to withdraw their cases and a compromise was negotiated. Radha went back to live with her husband, but their marriage never really took off. Every time they fought, he would get nasty about her going to the police. Ten years of a rocky marriage and two unhappy children later, they finally parted ways, each unable to reconcile the hurt that the other had felt when the law had been allowed into their lives.

The law is meant to protect us, prevent injustice and provide justice when we are faced with inequities. However, knowing how overworked the justice system is, we tend to abuse laws that were designed to protect. In recent years I have seen more abuse of Section 498A, the Domestic Violence Act and Anti-

Dowry legislation than can be explained away as chance occurrences. We cannot expect the courts to redress all our ego hassles and personal battles. Nor should we look for loopholes in the system that can be exploited to teach lessons to people we are angry with. The law cannot tell us how to be married. It can only tell us the circumstances under which marriages can be legally terminated. The police cannot be expected to play the role of marriage counsellors; they have plenty of more serious things to do. Once one partner appeals to the civil or criminal justice system to resolve inequities in the marriage, it is reasonable to conclude that such a marriage, even if it is forced to continue, can never plumb the depths of love, companionship and intimacy that a marriage should, unless both partners deal completely with the issues that prompted legal interference in the first place. For instance, in Radha's marriage, the real issues were the social and economic differences between the partners, the fact that a largish dowry had been paid, Pravin's reluctance to engage with his wife and the influence of Radha's father in her life. I ask you, can the courts of law be reasonably expected to deal with these issues?

17

Seeking Help

Asking for help, an absurdly simple thing to do on the face of it, is perhaps one of the most difficult tasks for many urbanised people today, ranking right up there with saying 'sorry'. We find it relatively easy to ask for help for the 'small stuff', but when it comes to things that really matter, it's really extraordinary how difficult it becomes. The easiest thing to do would be to dismiss this phenomenon as being caused by 'ego problems', a basket term that is gaining increasing currency in recent times. However, when we see people who are laid-back, self-effacing and far from egoistical, also resorting to the same behaviour, this explanation simply does not cut it. We need to dig just a little deeper than this.

Looking back at over two decades of being in the 'healing' profession, I can readily see that people sought my help most easily when I was a general medical practitioner, with much more difficulty when I was a clinical psychiatrist and with utmost awkwardness when I settled down to the practice of individual and couples psychotherapy. In other words, having a physical illness is perfectly acceptable when it comes to seeking help. When it comes to a diagnosable mental illness, the stigma associated with having such a problem does come in the way, but eventually, when the problem becomes unmanageable, a discreet visit to the mental health professional is still not considered improper. But when it comes to seeking help for 'non-illnesses' like marital and relationship problems, active inertia usually sets in.

As is well known, men find it hard to ask for help, unless they are employees of an enlightened organisation that pays for them to attend expensive seminars and workshops on sensitivity enhancement and the like. According to reports in Western literature, 96 per cent of those who seek the services of couples' therapists are women. Men enter the process only when they are compelled to—and with poorly-concealed reluctance at that. My experience in India is also similar. When I first started working with couples, nine times out ten it was the woman who first sought help. However, the good news is that in recent years, three times out of ten, it is the man who comes to see me first, whether or not his wife wants to accompany him. We are apparently well into the Age of the Metrosexual.

Put differently, it appears that one of the hallmarks of masculinity is the capacity to 'handle' everything—emotional or intellectual—by taking these matters in one's stride. Even if one doesn't know how to handle a situation, or one doesn't possess the wherewithal to deal with a crisis, one somehow bumbles through or 'wings' it. Revealing one's inability is unacceptable. Why should this be so? What is wrong with exposing one's difficulties or shortcomings? Is it not the imperative first step in managing one's problems, to acknowledge that they indeed exist, so one can confront them and deal with them?

The answers to these questions centre round a major fear in contemporary life: the fear of vulnerability, and the resultant conflict between emotional dependence and independence. The feeling in most peoples' minds tends to be that the more vulnerable one is, and the more one exposes that, the more dependent one becomes on others in the environment and, therefore, the more prone to these 'others' exerting control over and manipulating one. Many men therefore conclude, and erroneously, I may add, that the better option appears to be the quest for invulnerability. One of the manifestations of this is the reluctance, even refusal, to ask anyone for help. Although this evolved as a masculine trait, contemporary women too have included it in their decision-making repertoire, as part of a process of having to acquire masculine tools to enable them to compete in a man's world. The net result: Everyone aims to be invulnerable and independent of everybody else. Some people even do believe that they are.

If truth be told, those who believe this are deluding themselves. Nobody is truly independent or invulnerable. We are a highly social species, and as a result, will always be dependent on one another, whether we like it or not. The process of personal growth and development demands that we accept this reality and come to terms with it; the mature person is one who seeks to get comfortable with vulnerability, not to eliminate it. The sooner we recognise that we are all interdependent on each other and can be so with comfort, the better will we perform as a race.

So, next time we feel vulnerable, let us not attempt to be strong, silent types. Let us try to identify resources in our emotional and social environment that can assist us with solutions. To do this, we first need to learn to ask for help. Not indiscriminately of course. Let us choose our help-providers with care and discernment, and utilise their experience and expertise as best we can. For the benefit of the uninitiated, all our metros and most of our cities and larger towns have a fair number of psychiatrists, psychologists and counsellors who can help. A psychiatrist is a medical professional who has undergone post-graduate training in psychiatry, and usually uses a combination of medication and psychotherapy (helping the individual or couple find resolutions to their issues by talking through them); a clinical psychologist is a psychologist who has undergone post-graduate training in clinical psychology, is not licensed to prescribe medication but is trained to administer psychotherapy; and a counsellor is one who has undergone a two-year post-graduate degree in counselling and is equipped to counsel people with emotional difficulties. These apart, I have come across a variety of untrained 'counsellors' who have no formal training but do have a flair for obtaining people's confidences. They do not appear to follow any theory, and usually offer advice of the garden variety rather than professional counselling.

If I had my way, every couple would see a couples' therapist or a counsellor. This is simply because we have little or no training in marriage, but are expected to engage in this life-changing and often identity-threatening process using our factory-set defaults. No wonder we find the going rough. My personal suggestion is not to wait for serious problems to develop before seeing a counsellor. Go and see one, when even one of you feels you've hit a bit of a road-block or bottle-neck in your marriage. Maybe you will find a good counsellor with whom you can work out a solution to your problem. Can you handle it on your own? Perhaps you can. But you don't fix your mobile phone or laptop yourself, do you? As I see it, if you throw a child in the water, it will possibly learn to swim. But if the child had a swimming coach, it would probably learn to swim more efficiently. This is really what a counsellor can do for you. Be your 'marriage coach'.

If you are unsure of whom to go to, ask your family physician who may put you on to the right one. Whomever you choose, make sure you are comfortable with the person, for much of the success of the therapeutic process would depend on this. Don't expect them to come well recommended by patients, though. Most persons in our country who've gone through therapy feel too stigmatised to even acknowledge the fact, let alone pay encomiums to their therapist.

18

A Final Word

The first year of marriage can be an utterly charming experience. It can be an equally bewildering one if you do not possess the right mindset and the appropriate tools with which to get the best out of the new state of life you have entered. Unfortunately, marriage is one of the few institutions that one enters with absolutely no training, no manual to help you and a bundle of expectations—some clearly defined, but many only half-formed. What I have attempted to do in the preceding chapters is give you some idea of what you can do with your marriage to make it more manageable and malleable to your own needs, with due consideration to the needs of the new person you have chosen to co-navigate your life with. The idea is to make the experience less overwhelming than it needs to be, but at the same time to configure it in a manner that it meets the needs of both the protagonists.

You might wonder whether a book can accomplish all this. I did too, until I wrote my first book on marriage, and was pleasantly surprised to see how well it was received. Expecting people to resolve all their marital issues by merely reading a book would be foolish. But what I do expect to happen is that, once such a self-help book is read, it will jump-start a process of seeking solutions. Rather than believe that nothing can be done, readers will feel empowered to seek solutions by talking, listening, reading more books on the subject, and maybe even talking to a therapist. In other words, reading a self-help book could be a very vital first step in moving out of the *victim* mode that most of us fall into when faced with a crisis, to an *action mode* that gets us out of an emotional quagmire.

But let us not for a moment believe that a book can offer us neat and pre-packaged solutions. In this book I offer no prescriptions. I'm no messiah of marriage, nor am I a peddler of solutions. Every marriage is unique and what I've attempted to do in this book is to help a couple understand the dynamics of generic issues in the marriage. I've found that most marriages come unstuck mainly because neither partner has a starting point or a handle on the issues associated with the new reality that they find themselves in. This is all I've attempted to provide. The way I see it, when one is able to obtain an understanding of the dynamics of a relationship such as marriage, one is empowered to act more consciously and make more considered choices.

Without doubt, we live in a changing environment. The last few years have witnessed a sea change in how we approach and handle issues that are placed in our paths. Whatever slogan may be coined to define the new force that we call India, the fact is that contemporary realities and processes are now getting well entrenched in the minds of the new Indian. Naturally therefore, the New Indian Marriage is gradually replacing its older avatar. And frankly, I don't see this as a bad thing. The institution of marriage was getting a little complacent and was certainly in need of a bit of a shake-up. That it has responded to this need and undergone some internal tweaking and reformatting, has ensured its own survival in the face of inexorable social change.

The New Indian Marriage does, however, possess its own unique issues and bottlenecks. As one who has observed the changing face of Indian marriage from close quarters over the last quarter of a century, I have had the privilege of a ring-side seat during this period. I have attempted to distil and share with you some of the observations and inferences that such a seat has facilitated me to make. It is my hope that, if you use some of these, right at the beginning of your marriage, the Family Courts in the country may be less burdened, and will have to deal only with irreparable breakdowns and irreconcilable differences.

But to do this, you will have to work smart at owning your marriage and addressing the issues therein with clarity, rationality and self-assurance. This way, you can ensure that your marriage provides both you and your partner with the emotional fulfilment that marriage certainly can, provided it is configured appropriately. Hopefully, this book will help in this direction.

If you are one of those who sneaked a glance at the final chapter to see how it turned out, I am sorry to tell you that the butler didn't do it. You'll have to read the entire book to find out how your marriage can turn out. Here's wishing you a long and happily married life.